THE DARKNESS WHERE GOD IS

The Darkness
Where
God Is

Reconciliation and Renewal in
Northern Ireland

DAVID GILLETT

KINGSWAY PUBLICATIONS
EASTBOURNE

ISBN 0 86065 215 7

Front cover photo: Colour Library International

KINGSWAY PUBLICATIONS LTD
Lottbridge Drove, Eastbourne, E. Sussex BN23 6NT
Typeset by Nuprint Services Ltd, Harpenden, Herts.
Printed and bound in Great Britain by Collins, Glasgow.

Contents

Introduction: Above All, Pray

'Pray at all times in the Spirit, with all prayer and supplication. To that end keep alert with all perseverance, making supplication for all the saints' (Eph 6:18).

Some time ago I spoke to an ecumenical gathering in England and afterwards was speaking with one of the local Roman Catholic clergy. Like so many priests in England he is Irish, yet he confessed to a lack of concern about what was going on in Ulster. 'I suppose there's a kind of weariness about the situation—perhaps tied in with a bit of natural embarrassment on my part. I must confess that until tonight my wish has been that Northern Ireland would just drift out into the Atlantic ocean and get lost!'

It's an understandable reaction. On the many occasions on which I have spoken to English Christians about Northern Ireland I have found them to be suffering from a kind of prayer-paralysis. 'We have been praying for ten years and more—all we see on the TV seems to show that our prayers are not being answered. How can we go on praying? What, in fact do we pray for? Are there any answers? Is the situation really so insoluble as the politicians make out? What are the churches doing?'

The average Christian in England can find very few answers to these questions. I hope to be able to shed some light on them in what follows.

What I write is inevitably a personal reflection. It is based on my three years as a member of the community in the Christian Renewal Centre at Rostrevor in Northern Ireland. I tell something of this work in Chapter 7. For me these three years were the most challenging I have yet known. I am indebted to the Irish for all the love I received from them—both Catholic and Protestant, for all that I learnt about the victory of Christ against odds which, humanly speaking, seem insuperable. I have experienced, more than I dreamt possible, the results of centuries of division and bitterness. By God's grace I have also experienced in a wholly new dimension the power of repentance, forgiveness, love and reconciliation.

All these are now part of my life—they have changed me and I am deeply grateful to God and the Irish people for the privilege of sharing in their life for three years. I hope in what follows that my love and gratitude come through—it's certainly what I feel. But I cannot allow that to shackle some of the things I shall say. It is necessary, for instance, at times to tell the truth about the sectarian situation—and that is far from flattering. I only tell it because God's solution is based on the situation as it is, not on some gloss that we might wish to draw to make it seem less unpleasant.

As soon as one reflects in public on what God is doing in Northern Ireland it is inevitable that certain things come under the judgement of God's word—that would be true in any society. I have not avoided these issues when they have become clear to me.

My concern in writing this book is threefold. Firstly, that my Christian brothers and sisters n Ireland, both Roman Catholic and Protestant, will continue to look to God to hear what he is saying and have the courage to move forward—I am so grateful to God for my fellowship with some of the many who are daily committed to this prophetic task.

Secondly, I hope that any reader outside Ireland will ask first—how does this experience relate to me and my situation? The problems in Ireland are clearly visible to even the most insensitive outside (though their significance and complexity would baffle the most intelligent), but often the same attitudes, problems and sins are there in other societies though more disguised. I believe that just as the honour of God is at stake through what happens in Northern Ireland, so the situation is instructive for those who live elsewhere. It should make others ask, 'In what ways are these or similar problems deeply embedded in our own society?' In other words, unless we let the word of God judge us first we should never say 'Amen' when we see it pointed out in relation to someone else.

Thirdly, I hope this book will help people outside of the situation to pray for Ireland. I aim to help those who have not lived in Ireland to understand the history, the situation today and what it feels like, so that people can pray with more understanding. The images received via the television screen are inevitably too selective to provide a good back-cloth for our imagination as we pray. My aim also is to give examples of how God has been answering prayers over these last fourteen years so that you may have hope to go on—or possibly to start praying again.

This third aim is indeed my main reason for writing the book. I have agreed very reluctantly to put pen to paper in such an indelible and public fashion. Most authors in Northern Ireland confess the same. I do share the same reluctance as my fellow Christians in Ireland to tell some of the facts—I would rather some things were not told because they reflect on us all (though I have made a determined effort to resist 'washing dirty linen in public'). I am conscious of the debt I owe to the Irish church for the privilege of sharing with them for three years—it is a personal story and I am fearful of cheapening it. But above and beyond all this I have a deep conviction that the churches in the rest of the United Kingdom have a first-order duty to pray, and pray constantly, for their brothers and sisters in Northern Ireland.

What I have to say is no systematic treatise. There are many areas that are only briefly mentioned. The situation is too complex to give a complete analysis in a book of this size—and it would be beyond my competence to do so! I offer what follows as a series of windows into what it is like in Northern Ireland from the privileged position of having shared in it for three years.

The church in Ireland needs all of us who intercede for that land to pray from a position of confidence and victory in what Christ has done. I believe that it is the particular privilege and duty of Christians not personally involved in the situation to proclaim the victory of Christ in the spiritual realm, for 'we are not contending against flesh and blood, but against the principalities, against the powers, against the world rulers of this present darkness, against the spiritual hosts of wickedness in the heavenly places' (Eph 6:12). The more I have seen of the struggle 'on the ground' the more I have become aware of the spiritual battle that is going on. Most who read this are too far from Belfast, Derry, Armagh and Newry to be involved in the day-to-day outworkings of this struggle, but physical distance is no barrier to involvement in the spiritual battle. The prayer of God's people is vital—and that must be the prayer that is confident in Christ's victory.

Of the many prophecies given over these past years in Ireland one given at the Spiritual Renewal Leaders' Conference in September 1981 explains well the thrust of what God is doing. It provides an outline and basis from which our prayer can begin.

'You are to realize that the things that keep you apart, that prevent you entering into my purposes for this nation, are the very things that have been put to death on the cross. So as you find things in your heart rising up that you cannot cope with, you are to see that they have been nailed to the cross. Reckon yourselves dead to sin but alive through Christ. You have got to see that supernatural power has been released through my Son, and that you are not slaves. Even the things that you feel you will never break free from, these are the very things which have been put to death, because I need free men and women to fulfil my purposes. I need people who are free to hear my word and to obey it.... I have been speaking to you...in order to deliver you, to release you from all the history and tradition and bondage that that brings, and prejudices, in order that you may walk by faith. See that what you leave behind is pathetic compared to what I am setting before you. The things that seem so much part of you, when you lose them to receive what I have for you, you will breathe free. See, I have come to set you free. I have given you my Son; I have given you the power of Calvary and the power of the resurrection. You are resurrected by faith. You live by the power of an indestructible life, through Christ Jesus, my Son, so open your eyes this day and rejoice and be glad, give glory unto me, because, behold, I am doing a great thing. I am going to send a mighty revival to this land. I am preparing a people that can contain the power. I am preparing the people who will walk with me, be co-workers with me, as I move in great power in this land. No power can hold me back except my people.'

An Ancient Irish Prayer

Almighty and Merciful God,
who in days of old didst give to this land
the benediction of thy Holy Church;
withdraw not, we pray thee,
thy favour from us,

but so correct what is amiss,
and supply what is lacking,
that we may more and more
bring forth fruit to thy glory;
through Jesus Christ our Lord.

Amen.

1. A Spiritual Battle

It was the afternoon of the English Cup Final in 1982. I was listening to the commentary of extra-time on my car radio as I drove back from Dublin to my home in Northern Ireland. As the match ended—a 1–1 draw—I got down to thinking through the amazing hour I'd just spent in a hotel in Dublin.

I'd been talking with Al Ryan, one of the leading men in the Irish section of the Full Gospel Business Men's Fellowship. He is a short stocky man in his late forties from Waterford in the Irish Republic. I'd recorded our conversation and I played through the last part of this as I drove along. His closing words of confidence and hope were particularly striking. He was speaking of charismatic renewal and, in particular, of the work of the Full Gospel Business Men's Fellowship in Ireland.

> God brought in men from the UDA, the IRA and the UVF. People from North and South have come together. This is the work of God. Only God could bring Orangemen and IRA, Fianna Fail and Fine Gael[1] to sit down together at a meal and then give testimony to how Jesus Christ has changed their lives. This has to be God. The political leaders in both our nations have failed to bring about reconciliation and, at the end of the day, the only way it will happen is by men being reconciled first to God and then being reconciled with their brothers and

sisters in the same land. This is the way it's going to happen!

I am confident that this nation will be united. I believe God has shown me that. But it will not come about by killing. All killing is futile. Killing other human beings is just doing the work of Satan for him. We need to turn to prayer. If the whole nation would resort to prayer then the situation would be solved.

As I switched off the tape and drove on towards the border between North and South I reflected on how many times during the past three years I'd seen evidence of that reconciliation which Al was talking about. I was aware of our daily life in the community at the Christian Renewal Centre where we live, work and pray together in the unity that Jesus brings—Catholic and Protestant, Irish and English. I remembered the very first time that I saw a moment of reconciliation occur in the Renewal Centre. It was between a former sergeant in a Protestant paramilitary group and a Catholic farmer from the Republic. Neither had met before, and both of their backgrounds had conspired to fill them with suspicion, fear and hatred of one another. But in that meeting they sensed their unity in the Spirit and the love of Christ that unites more strongly than any other force can divide. It was a moving sight to see them both embrace as brothers together in God's family.

I certainly agreed also with what Al had said about prayer being the basis for any real way forward. My mind turned to those words of the Lord which came to King Solomon in a vision soon after the Temple had been completed. God was instructing Solomon about what his people should do when they face times of national calamity. 'If my people who are called by my name humble themselves, and pray and seek my face, and turn from their wicked ways, then I will hear from heaven, and will forgive their sin and heal their land' (2 Chron 7:14). This call to fasting, prayer and repentance has so often formed the basis of what we have seen God doing over these last years.

Shortly before arriving home at Rostrevor I drove past the spot where, three years before, eighteen British soldiers had been killed in an IRA ambush. It was on that same day that a bomb had killed Lord Mountbatten while he was on holiday in the West of Ireland. Al was right—*that* was doing Satan's work for him!

The more I have mulled over and prayed through that conversation with Al Ryan the more light has been shed on what is going on in Ireland. Al's is a very strange story. His conversion is as real as any other Christian I know—yet it is very unorthodox, even bewildering. To my theologically trained, evangelical outlook his story almost defies analysis. It certainly does not fit into any neat categories in which we often try to pigeon-hole the ways of God. But then my time in Ireland had showed me that God is too great to be pigeon-holed. Our theological and doctrinal systems must always be flexible enough to be moulded by something God does which is new to our experience. We are, of course, right to judge every new event by Scripture—but how often we discover as we do this that our previous understandings of Scripture have been limited by our past awareness of God! So now, to Al's story.

Al Ryan was born in the city of Galway on Ireland's Atlantic coast. His father was from Belfast, and his family had been driven out of their home by the sectarian troubles in the twenties. Al was baptized and brought up a Catholic attending a school run by the Christian Brothers.

He remembers that from about the time he was eight he had deep nationalistic ambitions—he longed to see Ireland united and completely free from the British. He was not actually taught these ideas; he imbibed them from the culture in which he was reared. This was a very religious culture though Al seemed destined from an early age to be no orthodox believer. As a lad he found it almost impossible to learn the teachings of the Christian faith. He was not a slow learner, in fact he was above average in every other subject. But when it came to learning his catechism, his mind seemed to go on strike. So much so that he was given extra tuition after school to prepare him for the pre-confirmation quizzing by the Bishop. But this special treatment seemed to be having very little effect.

On the Thursday before his confirmation he went to his interview with the Bishop. He could remember almost nothing, yet he would have to answer three questions. But, by an amazing stroke of good fortune Al was asked just one, 'Who is the Mother of God?' To an Irish Catholic that was probably the easiest question in the book, and he managed an acceptable answer!

The following Sunday he stepped forward for the laying on of hands at Confirmation and, as the Bishop prayed for the coming of the Holy Spirit, Al began to speak in a strange language. Anyone who knew their New Testament—and he didn't—would realize that it is perfectly normal to speak in tongues as a sign of the presence of God's Spirit—but it was to be over thirty years before Al was to understand the significance of this strange phenomenon that had happened to him. Down through the intervening years he would often find himself speaking in these strange languages—they seemed to come spontaneously in moments of joy and to be a source of strength and comfort in times of trouble and apprehension.

It was a confusing religious beginning for an eight-year-old boy—unlearned in some of the most basic truths of Christianity yet possessing one of the gifts of God's Spirit. His religious confusion was deepened further by his awareness of poltergeist activity and various other strange spiritistic experiences. It is not surprising that this confused state led him to give up church-going altogether. He stopped going soon after his confirmation and did not return until he was married nearly twenty years later.

Yet he was not without religion, for another cause, as strong as any traditional religion, was growing ever stronger year by year. By the early fifties a strong nationalistic fervour had so taken hold of his life that he got involved in the IRA. He was at this time working in Waterford and it was there that he recruited young men to form a local unit of the IRA. He organized training camps that included other units as well as his own and soon discovered that many of his cousins were also members. His family were playing a large part in the fifties border campaign which raged for six years in the southern part of Ulster.

Al Ryan's jobs in the IRA network included obtaining arms and ammunition, organizing expeditions and, at times, leading them into Northern Ireland. Often he transported arms across the border to his comrades in the North and was finally arrested for blowing up a railway bridge. For these activities he served nearly five years in jail.

By the time he was released from prison in 1962 the IRA command had called off the border campaign. He himself was becoming increasingly disillusioned by the basic drift to the left within the IRA. Marxism was quickly becoming the underlying philosophy and, internationally, they were very closely aligned with the Palestine Liberation Organization. Al himself was definitely not a communist and at the same time he had always been a strong supporter of Israel. It led in 1966 to his leaving the IRA.

It was to be only a temporary period of inactivity. When the troubles flared up again in 1969 he joined the newly formed non-Marxist Provisional IRA. Again he was heavily involved in gun-running, intelligence work, shootings and bombings in the North and public rallies in the South for the Provisionals' cause in Ulster. It was after speaking at one of these rallies that he was arrested and charged with inciting the defence forces in the Republic to hand over arms to the IRA.

He spent nine months in Mountjoy prison, and during his imprisonment his conscience began to trouble him. He soon found that he was unable to sleep because he was so disturbed by the thought of the bombings and the shooting in which he had been involved. Again and again he heard a voice saying to him, 'It's wrong, it's wrong.'

One particular night he was finding sleep totally impossible. The voice kept saying, 'It's wrong. It's wrong. It's wrong.' He began to wonder whether God was involved. Had he anything to do with this persistently nagging guilt that dominated all other thoughts? Eventually he burst out, 'God, if you're in this would you show me? If I've really gone wrong will you please do something about it?' With that he fell asleep almost immediately and woke the next morning refreshed. He felt a new sense of peace within himself. He could not understand what was happening but God was clearly beginning to re-order his life following that desperate plea of the night before. And so things continued for the next few weeks until a call in the middle of the night told him that he was being released that same day. He stepped out of the prison gates in the early morning and, as he walked down the long avenue to where his wife was waiting in the car, he heard a voice behind him, saying, 'Now, remember to keep the peace.' He looked back; perhaps it was a warder who had said that—but there was no one in sight, the avenue was deserted. 'Who said that?' he wondered. He was not yet able to recognize the sign of God at work in his life but he was aware of an undeniable sense of peace that was growing inside him.

He was determined not to lose this newfound experience of wellbeing, and he understood enough to know that he must break his links with the Provos. For four years he concentrated on building up his business again and managed to keep out of any further involvement with the paramilitary organizations. But still he did not recognize what God had done for him. He cleared out one demon, and in came another. He began to spend more and more time drinking with his business friends until eventually he acknowledged that he was an alcoholic. It was very nearly the last straw that ruined his marriage. His wife, Peggy, had suffered much during his time with the IRA but now his drinking was pushing her beyond the limit. She had several breakdowns over the years and the situation was becoming unbearable.

But God was not giving up on them yet! Two nuns had shown a loving concern for Al and his family. They were often in their house and one Friday evening they invited Peggy to go with them to the charismatic prayer meeting which they attended each week. For the next eighteen months Peggy went each Friday. She came to know the Lord and was baptized in the Spirit but Al understood very little of these things. He saw that Peggy began to read her Bible a lot, and she obviously knew her way around it. She seemed to understand what it was about, and she could even quote parts of it from memory. This puzzled Al greatly because it was not a Catholic way of doing things at all. The only conclusion he could draw was that his wife was learning it all from the Jehovah's Witnesses!

One Friday evening Al came home with a few drinks already inside him. When the two nuns came to call for Peggy on their way to the prayer meeting, Al thought he would quiz them a little.

'Tell me then, what happens at these Prayer Meetings?'

'If you're really interested, why don't you come along and see for yourself,' they replied.

'All right, I will!'

Quickly they arranged for a baby-sitter before he changed his mind. On the way to the meeting they persuaded him to agree to give it a try for four weeks. He agreed again. Very soon he was regretting his decision. He thought they were all mad! The evident enthusiasm, the hallelujah's, and the rest were all too much for him. Afterwards he was feeling very angry about the whole set-up. Nevertheless he returned the next week because he had made a promise.

It was on his third visit that God, who had been pursuing him down through the years, finally confronted him. As the meeting progressed Al sensed a brilliant shaft of light piercing the gathering. He himself felt a warmth throughout his body. 'What's happening to me? I wonder if this has anything to do with God?'

Just then a man stood up. 'I'm sorry for interrupting the meeting but I have a strong conviction that God wants me to say these few words for someone here tonight—*I am the Lord your God*'.

'Immediately,' Al recalls, 'I felt a bolt of power going right through my body. I knew it was God answering me.'

During the next few weeks he became absolutely convinced that God had met with him. He bought his first ever Bible and read it avidly. One evening about two months later he and Peggy were praying together before going to bed. She then retired and he stayed on praying alone, but very soon he was deeply burdened with remorse. He remembered how as a lad he had robbed the poor box in church. Then he remembered the shootings, the bombings and the others he had involved in trouble—some of them in prison, others already dead. It was a grim record of which he could only be deeply ashamed. There was no questioning the reality of his repentance. The sacrifice of Christ on Calvary could cover all his sin. As Jesus was hanging on the cross he had said to the penitent thief on the cross beside him, 'Today you will be with me in paradise.' When Al Ryan had turned in penitence from his sin, however black his past, he could be sure to find the same open acceptance from Jesus.

Yet there were voices within his mind at that moment which were saying exactly the opposite. 'Who do you think you are? God is not interested in you. You're fooling yourself. God would never have anything to do with someone like you.' He felt himself thoroughly condemned. He had turned to Christ but he did not experience the perfect freedom of which St Paul wrote: 'There is therefore now no condemnation for those who are in Christ Jesus.'[5]

Again God met with him and led him into that assurance of freedom and cleansing which is his gift to every child of God. He felt his hands being raised, palms upwards, and hands laid upon his head. Then he sensed two balls of flame placed one in each hand. At the same time he was conscious of a deep release of things long twisted and knotted up inside of him being set free. There was a deep sense of the presence of God and for about twenty minutes he praised God in tongues.

He ran upstairs to his wife, excited that God had met with him and brought such release and freedom. She pointed him to St Matthew's Gospel and the testimony of John the Baptist that Jesus would baptize his followers with the Holy Spirit and with fire.[6] Al had experienced that releasing and empowering of God's Spirit, he had known the deep cleansing work of Jesus, and he had also known a deliverance from all the demonic forces which had held such sway in his life down the years.

God, in his sovereign grace, had transformed Al Ryan and over the next few weeks he did a lot of thinking about the future. He heard clearly the call of God to leave behind everything in the world he had known and to follow Christ unreservedly. He knew it would mean losing all his friends, and facing endless ridicule. He knew his wider family would disown him. But he also knew that he had found a peace with God that he would not change for anything else.

Finally, he made an unconditional surrender to Christ. 'I will follow you,' he said. It was a wholehearted commitment to live totally under the Lordship of Jesus Christ. No other master could have any place at all. The only cause that could claim his absolute allegiance was the kingdom of God.

It had been no hasty meeting with God. At first glance, it had very little in common with a straightforward response at an evangelistic crusade! It had been a series of confrontations with his Maker over forty years during most of which he had rebelled against what God was wanting to do. Now, as he continues to grow as a Christian, Al can see the whole process and is the first to acknowledge the enormous change that it has made in his life.

All the hatred that was in me has gone. I had helped foster hatred and killing because I was so angry. Now all this has gone as though it had never been there. All my former friends were lost. None of them wanted me any more, even my relations disowned me.

Now I have a new life with new friends—far more than ever before. There's also the peace and contentment of God—I have no fear about tomorrow. I know it's just a case of trusting in God, doing the work of God, reading the Scriptures, and getting to know and understand him more deeply.

God has put a whole new world at my feet. He has delivered me from my alcohol problem, he's healed me from smoking as well as a sinus problem and my life now is given over to doing whatever he wants me to do. I know I'm called particularly to work for reconciliation in the nation and in reconciliation with other nations. I'm specially concerned to pray and work for reconciliation between Ireland and England. But most of all I want to bring others to Christ so that they are reconciled to God—this is the most important thing in the world today.

What God is doing in Ireland today is similar to what Jesus did when he rode into Jerusalem on Palm Sunday. The Jews thought he would throw out the Romans and change the whole political scene for them. He didn't—but he gave them a far greater victory on the following weekend. I've seen this in my own life. I've had a resurrection, a new birth, I'm born again now and I live first for God, then for my family, and then for my country. What God has done for me he can do for anyone else.

As I have gone through Al Ryan's story again and again it strikes me that it is an example in one man of the major conflict that rages in Ireland—the conflict for man's soul, the fight for his allegiance.

It is a conflict that stems from a perfectly right longing on the part of the majority of the Irish people to be free from British rule. It has become a basic principle of British parliamentary democracy that all peoples have the right to freedom and national self-determination. What has so often happened is that this fully acceptable human aspiration has been taken over by a demonic form of a nationalistic spirit which works through irrational fears, deep bitterness, and cruel violence. And the same is true on the other side of the divide in Northern Ireland today. It is a just cause that the Northern Protestants should want to retain their constitutional links with Great Britain. Yet demonic forces have just as clearly played on these aspirations to create the same ugly forms of fear, bitterness and violence.

Ireland was once known as 'the land of saints and scholars'. A contemporary observer would give a very different description. It is as though the devil is seeking to destroy what, in the past, has been so much used by God. So powerfully has the demonic evil of hatred and violence warped what God has done in Ireland's long history that she has become a by-word among the nations. The honour of God is at stake. It is not merely a human battle. At its deepest level it is a question of the allegiance of human hearts, and ultimately of the honour of Almighty God.

2. Captives of History

The average Englishman's ignorance about Ireland is immense. Whereas the Irish have for centuries been constantly aware of what goes on in England, the English, by contrast, have been relatively unaware of what is going on in Ireland except when trouble has flared up particularly badly. Consequently the Englishman has viewed Ireland about once in a generation and inevitably without any real understanding of the context. It is no wonder that what is seen on the television today seems bewildering to many. *With* a knowledge of the historical background the Irish question is tortuous enough; *without* such contextualization the conflict seems totally incomprehensible.

This lack of understanding leads to inadequate and naive responses. There is the cry of exasperation: 'Let's bang their heads together—that's what they need!' It is a reaction very like the inept response of a bewildered relative having to cope with a member of their family who is suffering from a nervous breakdown. 'Come on, there's nothing wrong with you, just snap out of it!' Of course, there is something *very* wrong deep within the person's mind, often affected by what has been going on for years—and probably unknown to the exasperated relative. It is similarly naive and inept of the English to respond in that way to the troubled state of the Irish people.

It is the same lack of understanding which leads many others to adopt the position of the injured party. To those who see Ireland only from the perspective of their own lifetime it is easy to think of the British as the previously uninvolved 'goodies' who went over to Northern Ireland in 1969 to help clear up the mess that 'they' had made. As the British forces' death role continues to rise the cry is heard, 'We have done our bit, now let's leave them to it!' The briefest historical understanding shows the total inadequacy of such a position.

At worst, for many English, knowledge of the Irish is confined to what they learn from Irish jokes! But generally the feeling is that there is nothing to learn. 'They're the same as us except they speak with a brogue.' This fails to explain how complex are the historical roots which have created a society of many strands, all of which have fundamental differences from those which have formed the English people.

The first and great difference to be acknowledged is that, whereas the English today have very little historical consciousness, the Irish—both Catholic and Protestant—still live very aware of the past. Recently I played host in July to some English visitors to Northern Ireland. The Union Jacks were much in evidence in the Protestant areas and I explained that this was in readiness for the celebrations to take place on July 12th which mark the Protestant victory at the Battle of the Boyne. My guest had not heard of this battle (and, in this, he is not unique among Englishmen!) but assumed that it must have taken place sometime earlier this century. He was amazed to hear that the battle in question had been fought in 1690. 'It's ridiculous! why on earth haven't they forgotten by now something that happened three hundred years ago?' Regrettable it may seem, but the reality is that, in a manner of speaking, the Battle of the Boyne is still going on. People in both communities feel under threats similar to those their forebears experienced centuries ago. King Billy is not just a former hero or ogre (according to your particular viewpoint) but he represents a conflict that is still going on. It has never been resolved, either in total victory by one side or the other, or in a lasting peace and reconciliation.

In a sense, the Irish are captives of history, and that not because of some kind of romantic or wistful love of glories that are past (like steam train enthusiasts) but because historical events still mould the present to a highly significant degree. Robert Kee aptly concluded his television history of Ireland with the observation that blame for the situation in Northern Ireland as we experience it today 'should be laid not at the door of the men of today but of history'.[1] There is evident truth in these words for, given a different history, there would not be the sectarian violence to which we have grown so accustomed in the more recent past. For instance, the republican cause is no doubt correct, at least in some cases, when it claims that the young men in prison today for terrorist offences are not ordinary criminals—they would not have broken the law were it not for the imperialist domination (as they see it) under which they live. It is surely right that some of the blame for today's shootings and bombings should go to those who created the situation. But equally clearly this does not exonerate any of us today. However moulded we might be by our history we are still accountable for our own actions.

It is important, then, to take a look at the history itself. This can only be done here in outline. For those who want to delve into the subject more deeply, the books mentioned in the list for further study will make fascinating reading. What is important is that we begin to *feel* the significance of different events in history as they are *felt* by people in Ireland today. Only by entering into this history can we begin to understand contemporary attitudes, fears and longings.

The political relationship between England and Ireland stretches back for eight hundred years. During this time it has been the most recurring problem that the government in London has had to face and, until the present century, England has always seen this relationship in terms of lordship. Ironically, it all began at the request of the Pope—perhaps significantly the only Englishman ever to occupy the papal throne. He was Nicholas Breakspear, a monk from St Albans, known as Pope Adrian IV. He requested King Henry II of England to bring Roman order to the rather unruly and independent-minded Irish Church. The papal Bull, Laudabiliter (1155) granted lordship of Ireland to the English king:

> We do hereby declare our will and pleasure that, with a
> view to enlarging the boundaries of the church, refraining
> the downward course of vice, correcting evil customs and
> planting virtue, and for the increase of the
> Christian religion, you shall enter that island and
> execute whatever may tend to the honour of God and the
> welfare of the land; and also that the people of that land
> shall receive you with honour and revere you as their Lord.

'What a relief!' claims the Englishman. 'At least our beginnings in Ireland were for good reasons, whatever the subsequent history.' Alas, there is no such way out of our eight-hundred-year responsibility. Henry did nothing about the Pope's request for fifteen years and when he did take an army to Ireland it had very little to do with a concern for the Church's purity or the salvation of souls. His aim was to put down a local ruler whose power had increased to such an extent that he could effectively challenge the lordship of the King of England within Ireland. It is this political note, to do with the security of the realm of England, that has been a dominant theme in succeeding centuries. It has usually been the fear that Ireland might provide an easy launching pad for hostile European powers to open up a second front in any war against England. It is a fear that occupied Winston Churchill in the second world war when Southern Ireland was a neutral power.

The first four hundred years of English rule up to the time of the Protestant Reformation, was a period which saw a series of spasmodic attempts to establish more effective control over Ireland, interspersed with years of relative neglect and uninterest. For most of the time effective power was in the hands of one or other of the local Earls; when these grew too powerful for comfort they were dealt with by the English monarch of the day.

The Reformation in England marks the beginning of a new chapter in Anglo-Irish relations. In 1534 the Earl of Kildare, the most powerful of the Irish nobility rebelled against Henry VIII partly on the grounds that, as Henry had been excommunicated by the Pope, he no longer retained the lordship of Ireland which in itself had been the gift of the Pope to a faithful Catholic monarch. The Earl failed in his attempt to challenge the rule of the English king and was executed for high treason at Tyburn in 1537. Four years later the Irish parliament was induced to declare Henry VIII, 'King of this land of Ireland, as united annexed and knit forever to the imperial crowns of the realm of England.'

Ireland remained largely unaffected by the Protestant Reformation. At first, under Henry VIII, the Irish Church did not object too much to what looked like 'Catholicism without the Pope'. After all it had been the English with whom the Pope had sided originally. The Irish had tended to guard jealously the Irish identity of their Church. It was when the Protestant doctrines followed the royal supremacy that there was strong resistance from the majority of clergy and laity. There was no powerful reform movement in Ireland like the one in England that gave a fundamantal

theological significance to the Reformation here. Consequently, the Book of Common Prayer, imposed by Act of
Parliament in Ireland as well as in England, was largely
unused across the Irish Sea. It was not only the new
doctrines and new services that offended but what, to the
majority of the faithful, was a new language.

No longer were the services in the old Latin with which
they were familiar. The authorities staunchly resisted the
idea of translating the Prayer Book into Irish, which most of
the Irish people spoke. The language was English, which
was largely unknown and, moreover, the language of a
foreign ruler who was seeking to impose new Protestant
doctrines on Irish Catholics. In 1560 the Irish Parliament
passed the Act of Uniformity and only two of the Irish
Bishops refused to take the Oath of Supremacy. In practice,
this was rarely enforced, the Book of Common Prayer
generally unused, and the Church in Ireland largely
unaffected by the Protestant Reformation. The English
thus complicated the future history of Ireland by failing to
be thorough in what they set out to do. This tendency to
adopt policies which are then only partially implemented is
the continuing saga of English rule throughout the centuries.

Following the Reformation, the Pope had, perforce,
changed sides. For four hundred years the papacy had been
England's ally in its domination of Ireland. Now, as a result
of the Reformation in England, Catholic Pope and Catholic
Ireland stood together. Four hundred years later when
Pope John Paul II made the first ever papal visit to Ireland
he paid tribute to this connection. 'Many are indeed the
bonds that unite your country to the See of Peter in Rome.
From the earliest beginnings of Christianity in this land, all
through the centuries until the present day, never has the
love of the Irish for the Vicar of Christ been weakened, but
it has flourished as an example for all to witness.' In fact,
John Paul II overstated the case for, before the Reformation,

there were many examples of a lack of 'love of the Irish for the Vicar of Christ'. Perhaps the Pope's gratitude can stand unchallenged because of the extremely zealous way in which Ireland has increasingly stood with Rome over the last four centuries.

It is at the beginning of the seventeenth century that Ulster, the most northerly of Ireland's four ancient provinces, comes to the forefront of Anglo-Irish relations. Ulster had rarely figured in the first four hundred years of English rule; it would gradually grow in dominance in the second four centuries until it became the 'thorn in the flesh' for England.

Previously, the main English settlement had been around the Dublin area; here the English rule was strongest and Protestantism more securely established. The area around Dublin where English rule was most effective was called the Pale of Dublin; beyond the Pale (hence the popular expression) security could not regularly be guaranteed. Ulster was way 'beyond the Pale'; it was strong Gaelic territory and almost exclusively Roman Catholic. Its resistance to the dominance of Protestant England was led by the Earls of Ulster. Eventually, in 1603, they were defeated by Elizabeth I to whom they swore loyalty. But, four years later, realizing that they were only puppets of the English Queen and no longer effective masters in their own house, they left Ireland for voluntary exile in France. The English government, under its new King, James I, determined to secure Ulster against any future rebellion following the flight of the Earls. He chose to do this by a policy of plantation.

In general terms, this meant that, from 1610–1630, the English 'planted' Protestants on land confiscated from the Irish. The Protestants came in two basic varieties—Anglicans from England and Presbyterians from Scotland. In these few years were laid the foundations of Ulster's problems in the twentieth century. Again, the situation is as complex as it is today because the original plantation policies (however unfortunate the concept) were never implemented with the thoroughness with which they were conceived.

As a result of the plantations there were now three identifiable groups of people in Ulster. First, there were the Gaelic race who were poor, politically powerless, robbed of most of their land, and staunchly Catholic. Secondly, there were the Scottish Presbyterians who were the small farmers and merchants. Thirdly, there were the English who belonged to the established Episcopalian Church. Although these were the smallest group it was they who owned most of the wealth and wielded all of the power.

In her life of James I, Antonia Fraser asserts that he 'had not the faintest understanding of the history, hopes and fears of the Irish people.'[2] It is, of course, easy to see this with hindsight, and many figures in history are thus judged more harshly than they deserve according to the accepted norms of their own day. Nevertheless, it remains true that from the mix created by the plantation policy in Ulster came the attitudes that have survived and often grown more noticeable in the succeeding centuries. The Catholic Irish, not unnaturally, felt aggrieved at being so harshly dispossessed and made a subject people under new masters in their ancient land. The seeds of inevitable rebellion had been sown. The new settlers, surrounded by these dispossessed and often angry Irish, quickly adopted a siege mentality. Consequently, they fortified their estates and farms and were, from the beginning, a very security-conscious community; their newfound possessions and the prosperity they brought would need defending forever if they were not to be lost.

When Charles I became King the seeds of conflict, arising from his father's plantation policy, were growing even stronger. Such problems were not, however, his prime concern. He had increasing trouble in working with his parliament in England which led to the Civil War in 1642. The conflict between king and parliament in the years prior to the English Civil War was yet one more factor which contributed to the ferment in Ireland. In 1641 this erupted in the Irish Rebellion that lasted throughout the decade. It was at its most vehement and bloody in the northern province of Ulster.

The history of this period is so confusing that it is almost impossible to unravel all the strands. The Irish factions and the warring parties in England and Scotland during the Civil War were continually jostling each other. However, two things clearly emerge from the confusion. First, notwithstanding the exaggeration and propaganda, some of which was officially sanctioned by the Protestant Parliament in Dublin, there were many cruel massacres of northern Protestant settlers perpetrated by the native Irish. Secondly, a major conflict in Ireland, was, for the first time, a fight between Catholic and Protestant.

The massacre has become part of the folk lore of Ulster Protestants. It is still remembered on some of the Orange banners paraded on July 12th. Most notable perhaps is the banner that depicts the massacre at Portadown in November 1641 when one hundred Protestants, men, women and children were herded together on the bridge and then thrown to drown in the river beneath. Those who looked likely to survive were clubbed to death by the rebels. For some time afterwards it was claimed that the ghostly form of a brutalized woman rose from the river crying, 'Revenge, Revenge!'

Myth and history have thus combined in the folk memory of Ulster Protestantism. The myths often inject into the facts far more potency and significance than they would carry by themselves. Although this rebellion happened at a time when the Protestants were still a minority in Ulster, the siege mentality persists to the present day when now the Protestants are in the majority in the Province. It was the events of the decade in the middle of the seventeenth century which irrevocably divided the Irish population into two nations within the one island and the most easily distinguishable characteristic would always be their respective religious traditions, Catholic or Protestant.

This division between the two sides, and particularly their religious differences, was further deepened in 1649 by the advent of the Commonwealth army led by Oliver Cromwell himself. Cromwell, proclaimed in the English Parliament, Lord Lieutenant of Ireland, crossed the Irish Sea for what he saw as a Christian crusade. He believed he was going to Ireland by divine providence and he told his army before embarking at Bristol that they were like the Israelites of old who had entered Canaan to rid it of its idolatrous inhabitants. His main military objective was to secure Ireland firmly within his control so that it could not be used as an easy back-door entry for hostile armies from the continent.

Cromwell was a very successful and ruthless soldier as many in England had already discovered at the cost of their lives. He held to the Old Testament conviction of the need to eradicate what he saw as dangerous and ungodly elements—they must not be allowed to continue as a festering and polluting presence within the body politic. The King of England had been executed as a result of this thoroughness on Cromwell's part and the Irish were about to see its results throughout their land. Cromwell saw his Irish campaign as the final and most radical battle to establish the puritan commonwealth. 'I had rather be overrun,' he declared, 'with a cavalierish interest than a Scotch interest; I had rather be overrun with a Scotch interest than an Irish interest; and I think of all, this is the most dangerous.'

First came the massacre of Drogheda. This has gone down as one of the most potent events in the myth-history of the Catholic Irish community. It corresponds to the Irish Rebellion of 1641 in the Protestant historical-consciousness. Ever since there have been two versions of Irish history, both being added to in each succeeding generation, and the version which any child is taught has depended on whether the school he attended was Catholic or Protestant. The danger is obvious—'your facts' are often given exaggerated and symbolic importance. 'Their facts' are played down, even ignored. Dialogue is impossible on such a basis as there is no agreement on the fundamental facts. It is nearly impossible to listen. The general substitute has been to proclaim your own story loudly for your own benefit and this is one of the major cultural significances of the traditional parades and demonstrations. It says to your side, 'Lest we forget.' The secondary effect of such parading of sectarian history is to inflame the other community.

The demythologization of Irish history is a crucial task, though a difficult one, because myth and symbol have been intertwined with fact almost before the dust has settled. But the attempt must be made—and particularly with what happened at Drogheda in 1649.

Cromwell was a disciplined army commander who believed in fighting according to the strict rules of siege warfare accepted by all parties at the time—though they seem horribly cruel to our more liberal outlook. This accepted procedure (the 'Geneva Convention' of the day) was that, if a garrison surrendered, its defenders should be spared, but if they refused to surrender then, if defeated, the besieging army should put the garrison to the sword. True to this principle, Cromwell offered terms of surrender to the Catholic armies who were defending Drogheda. The garrison commander, by one of history's ironies an English

Catholic, signified that his troops were unanimous in their resolution to perish rather than surrender the town. The consequent assault was costly for Cromwell's army and, as he wrote to the Speaker of the English Parliament, he ordered his men to kill the whole garrison, 'and indeed being in the heat of action, I forbade them to spare any that were in arms in the town, and I think that night they put to the sword about two thousand men.' The army, however, were less scrupulous than Cromwell, and there were many civilians including priests who perished in Drogheda. Sadly, it was even worse at Wexford later in the campaign.

On completion of his Irish crusade Cromwell banished the Catholic landlords to the poor lands of the extreme West of Ireland in what was the largest Government-directed movement of population these islands have known. The rich lands thus vacated, were given to Cromwell's men as reward for services rendered. Following this Cromwellian redistribution, the combined English policies of resettlement that covered the first half of the seventeenth century had left only 22% of Irish land in Irish hands.

Inevitably Cromwell is a hero in the Protestant con-sciousness. To the Catholic, he is a curse. His military victories paved the way for his rigorous anti-Catholic measures to be enforced. When negotiating terms of surrender with the Governor of New Ross he made clear that he would allow freedom of conscience to all his peoples, 'but if by liberty of conscience you mean the liberty of exercising the mass, I judge it best to use plain dealing, and to let you know, where the Parliament of England have power, that will not be allowed of.'

Cromwell saw the whole Irish campaign as an outworking of the justice of God on the Irish for the rebellion of 1641. After the sacking of Drogheda he wrote, 'I am persuaded that this is a righteous judgement of God upon those barbarous wretches, who have imbrued their hands with much innocent blood.' This view that sees military action as a direct way of promoting the cause of Christ has been a recurring belief at the heart of the Irish problem. While never becoming the major factor it is still used today at times as justification for both Catholic and Protestant para-military activity.

It is a case of New Testament 'means' being pursued by Old Testament 'methods'. This bastard mixture is far from the mind of Christ who on the night he was arrested said to Peter who had drawn his sword to attack Jesus' enemies, 'Put your sword back into its place; for all who take the sword will perish by the sword' (Mt 26:52; Jn 8:11). It is not only Ireland that has been affected by this unchristian view of Christianity. Similar theories lay at the heart of the Crusades and many other events in the history of Christendom. The only difference is that the effects of such a bastard Christianity continue to mould life in twentieth century Ireland when nearly all traces of it have disappeared in most other parts of the world. It is a sobering thought that the most thorough-going exponent of this Christian militarism on Irish soil was the Lord Protector of England —probably the most convinced evangelical ruler this country has known!

For the next few decades the sores continued but there was no new conflict produced by the Restoration of the monarchy under Charles II in 1660—in fact this was a time of relative stability and economic growth. The Restoration did, of course, bring the return of Episcopacy (abolished during the days of the Commonwealth). In 1661 the Church of Ireland became the established church in Ireland, even though the Episcopalians were a relatively small minority within Ireland. As in England this meant that Protestant dissent incurred penalties in law, though less stringent than those that governed Catholics. Over the years this made its mark on Presbyterians who have always formed the largest group within Ulster Protestantism. It has produced one of the less recognized, though nonetheless powerful attitudes that continue to govern much in Northern Protestantism. Robert Kee expresses the link between past and present: 'Though Presbyterians are of course no longer penalized as dissenters, the pyschological tradition of that sort of independence of spirit vigorously survives today as a political force. The Presbyterian determination to pursue what they see as *their* interest, both material and spiritual, figures continuously through the Irish history of the next three hundred years and more, and is one of the principal factors in the contemporary situation.'[3] Today this tradition can be seen very markedly in Ian Paisley and his followers. They are of course staunchly Protestant and strongly non-Irish as their Ulster forefathers were. They also exhibit what to many seem contradictory traits; they are pro-British and loyal to the Crown while at the same time displaying a deep-seated and often unconscious antipathy towards the English. The former comes from the need to be Loyal Unionists in the face of Home Rule republicanism; the latter stems from the penal days under the dominant English establishment.

The notable event that has passed into Catholic consciousness, from the reign of Charles II, occurred in 1681. Anti-Catholic feeling was running high in England. People feared that, because of their submission to the Pope, Catholics were inevitably disloyal to the Crown. As part of the general panic produced by this fear, Archbishop Oliver Plunkett, the Roman Catholic Archbishop of Armagh, and Primate of Ireland was arrested. He was brought to England, imprisoned, charged with high treason and executed. It is generally agreed to have been a gross miscarriage of justice. Some Catholics may have been disloyal and dangerous political agitators but the Archbishop was a peace-loving man of unimpeachable loyalty. He has become one of the most powerful symbols of anti-British attitudes among Irish Catholics. He has been venerated throughout the centuries and was finally canonized in 1975. Pope John Paul II gave his sanction to this veneration when he addressed the Irish at Drogheda in September 1979.

> *I have kept the faith.* That has been the ambition of the Irish down the centuries through persecution and through poverty, in famine and in exile, you have kept the faith. For many it has meant martyrdom. Here at Drogheda, where his relics are honoured, I wish to mention one Irish martyr, Saint Oliver Plunkett.... As bishop he preached a message of pardon and peace. He was indeed the defender of the oppressed and the advocate of justice, but he would never condone violence.... As a martyr for the faith, he sealed by his death the same message of reconciliation that he had preached during his life. In his heart there was no rancour, for his strength was the love of Jesus, the love of the Good Shepherd who gives his life for his flock. His dying words were words of forgiveness for all his enemies.

Nearly ten years after the martyrdom of Oliver Plunkett the Protestants gained their most potent historical symbols of all—and again it was largely as the result of a domestic English struggle. In 1688 the Catholic King, James II, was replaced by the Protestant Dutch Prince, William of Orange. James II fled to Ireland where the Catholic Irish rallied to his cause and the Protestants fiercely resisted him.

The most famous example of Protestant resistance was in the siege of loyal Protestant Derry. The city's governor was on the point of surrendering to the Jacobite army when a group of thirteen young apprentices slammed the gates against the invading Catholics and survived a long siege of thirteen weeks. When asked by the besieging troops to surrender their reply, which is still heard today, was terse and to the point, 'No surrender.' Many thousands died in the city during the course of the siege and eventually the English Protestant ships, which had been at hand for many weeks, broke through and relieved the city. Each year in Northern Ireland the 'No Surrender' principle is affirmed in the Apprentice Boys' marches on August 12th.

The siege of Derry also contained two other factors which highlight continuing attitudes in Ulster. Some of the leading Protestants in the city, including the commander of the garrison Lt. Col. Robert Lundy, were in favour of opening the gates to James' army. The popular outcry against Lundy was such that he had to flee the city in disguise. Today the name 'Lundy' is still applied to any who 'go soft', who weaken in the resolve to go to all lengths to defend the Protestant cause. Also, long memories still recall the weeks during which the British ships stood off and let the Ulstermen sweat out the siege on their own. There continues to this day the feeling that, although the Ulster Protestant can look to the British for a certain degree of support, they must always be prepared for the day when they must go it alone.

In June of the next year, 1690, the Protestant King William landed at Carrickfergus, just north of Belfast, and the two armies met on the River Boyne, a few miles from Drogheda. James and his Catholic troops were decisively beaten. This victory of King William III, formerly a Prince of the Orange Free State, adopted as King in England because of his impeccable Protestant record, thus gave a colour to the Protestant cause. It is the Orangemen who march on July 12th to celebrate the victory of King Billy; the triumph of the Orange over the Green. But it is not just important as a symbol for the Protestant community and their identity, it has had a decisive political effect on the subsequent history of Ireland. The supremacy of Protestants, though always outnumbered massively by the Catholic population continued until the declaration of the Irish Free State in 1921. The heirs of the dominant Protestant minority have lived on in the Unionist tradition of Northern Ireland as the majority community to the present day. The Battle of the Boyne is not merely a historical memory; for the inhabitants of Northern Ireland it still determines the present situation.

The succeeding centuries have added nothing substantially new to the political situation but the animosities were deepened considerably by various events. The penal laws against Catholics in the first half of the eighteenth century left deep feelings about the injustice of British rule. The totally inadequate response of the British government to the Irish peasants during the potato famine of 1845–48 has left an indelible mark on the Irish character. It is the Irish equivalent to the Jewish holocaust. A million died and another million emigrated to find a new life in the freedom of America. It is some of their descendants who today provide much of the American money that funds the IRA.

As parliamentary government in Westminster gradually took over more and more of the powers of monarchy the situation lost none of its insolubility of former years. Often British politicians showed a marked lack of understanding as well as anger over the Irish question. Prime Minister William Pitt declared in the House of Commons in January 1799, 'Ireland is subject to great and deplorable evils which have a deep root, for they lie in the situation of the country itself—in the present character, manners and habits of the inhabitants—in their want of intelligence, or in other words, their ignorance.' In his exasperation Pitt mouthed words which many Englishmen are still tempted to utter today. The blindness in such statements is in the British failure to acknowledge its own major role in creating the situation.

The history of British rule in Ireland has been an unhappy one. The repeated tendency has been to forget the issue as soon as it calmed somewhat and then to employ short term measures to quell any immediate crisis as it arose. The fundamental sore was always avoided—probably because its nature was rarely recognized. Paul Johnson summarizes these unsuccessful attempts of succeeding generations of British ministers—'Most of these men failed because Ireland was merely a passing episode in otherwise fruitful lives of public service and creative labours. But most of them accepted the fundamental misconception to which even the more enlightened British statesman and pundits have clung, that if only Britain gave Ireland justice, prosperity and wise government, the British connection would be accepted by her people. Alas, it is of the essence of wise government to know when to absent itself. Britain has learnt by bitter experience in Ireland that there is no substitute for independence.'[4]

William Gladstone was the first British politician to break the mould and to opt decisively for Home Rule as *the* solution to the Irish question. Twenty years before becoming Prime Minister, he wrote to his wife, 'Ireland, Ireland, that cloud in the west, that coming storm, the minister of God's retribution upon cruel and inveterate and but half atoned injustice.' He sought to understand the whole situation rather than react irrascibly to its particular manifestation of the moment. When he finally became Prime Minister he began by seeking to lessen the tension in the situation. In 1869, one year after becoming Prime Minister, he carried through Parliament the bill that disestablished the Church of Ireland, thus removing all the inbuilt privileges of the minority Anglican population which for two centuries had been a major irritant to Catholics and Presbyterians. He proceeded to open up education to Roman Catholics and introduce land reform but gradually came to realize that Home Rule, increasingly being advocated by politicians from Ireland, was the *only* step radical enough to solve the situation. But Gladstone was way ahead of the majority in both Houses of Parliament and British public opinion in general. His Home Rule Bill of 1886 was defeated.

By the turn of the century the 'Irish problem' to all intents became the 'Ulster problem'. Home Rule seemed inevitable to an increasing number, but to the Protestant majority in the northern province of Ulster this was totally unacceptable. Edward Carson, leader of the Unionist Party in Ulster rallied support against Home Rule. Their slogan was 'Home Rule is Rome Rule' and their battle cry, 'No Surrender.' In September 1911 Carson told a rally of fifty thousand men that in the event of a Home Rule Bill reaching the statute book they must immediately form from among themselves a government for the Protestant Province of Ulster. Four months later in January 1912 the Ulster Volunteer Force was formed with a hundred thousand men which demonstrated that, if necessary, they would defend Protestant Ulster by force.

To show the strength of feeling in Ulster the Protestant population was invited to sign a solemn covenant against Home Rule on September 28th 1912 in Belfast City Hall. The Covenant document was placed on a table covered with the Union Flag and William of Orange's standard from the Battle of the Boyne stood behind. 471,414 Ulstermen signed what was called 'Ulster's Solemn League and Covenant'. It read:

> Being convinced in our consciences that Home Rule would be disastrous to the material well-being of Ulster as well as of the whole of Ireland, subversive of our civil and religious freedom, destructive of our citizenship and perilous to the unity of the Empire, we, whose names are underwritten, men of Ulster, loyal subjects of His Gracious Majesty King George V, humbly relying on the God whom our fathers in days of stress and trial confidently trusted, do hereby pledge ourselves in solemn Covenant throughout this our time of threatened calamity to stand by one another in defending for ourselves and our children our cherished position of equal citizenship in the United

Kingdom and in using all means which may be found necessary to defeat the present conspiracy to set up a Home Rule Parliament in Ireland. And in the event of such a Parliament being forced upon us we further solemnly and mutually pledge ourselves to refuse to recognize its authority. In sure confidence that God will defend the right we hereto subscribe our names.

Partition was clearly becoming the only way forward but the whole issue was put into cold storage with the advent of the First World War. This however did not satisfy the more militant republicans in the South and in 1916 Padraig Pearse and James Connolly led the Irish Republican Brotherhood in the Easter Rising in Dublin. They held out against the British for nearly a week, and at the time received surprisingly little support from the populace at large. However the executions of the leaders, and the subsequent internment without trial of many others, led to a groundswell of hardening anti-British feeling which led to several years of bloody conflict. It was in this period that the IRA was formed to fight a guerrilla campaign against the British Imperial forces in Ireland.

This long and bitter struggle finally decided Lloyd George's government to grant limited independence to Ireland—they were granted dominion status as the Irish Free State. The 1921 Government of Ireland Act gave the six counties of Northern Ireland their own parliament and they remained part of the United Kingdom.

This arrangement was thought by some politicians to be temporary but clearly the Protestant majority in Ulster had decided otherwise. They had settled for partition as second best to the whole of Ireland remaining British and they would never make any further concession.

The Free State, which became a Republic in 1949 was largely a Catholic State; Northern Ireland was the Protestant equivalent. In 1934 Sir James Craig, who was Northern

Ireland's first Prime Minister, declared at Stormont, 'All I boast is that we have a Protestant Parliament and a Protestant State.' To our ears this sounds unacceptably partisan and exclusivist: it is only fair to point out that the Prime Minister was not so much declaring ascendancy over the minority Catholic populations in the North as acknowledging what he saw as the Protestants' fair share. The Catholics had the Free State and the Protestants had Northern Ireland. The argument went that if Catholics wanted to live in a Catholic State then they should move to the South.

The majority of Catholics in Ulster said in effect, 'But we don't want to move, this is our home and it has been for centuries.' The Catholic minority is sizeable—one third of the population of the Province. During the fifty years of exclusively Protestant rule in the Unionist Ascendancy this Catholic third were undoubtedly disadvantaged. Gerrymandering meant that Catholics were programmed to be poorly represented in local government with a consequent 'raw deal' in housing and public amenities. The policy of Protestants, who were the main employers, to employ only Protestants, while far from universal was widespread. It was the campaign against this lack of Civil Rights in 1968 which led to the present conflict in Northern Ireland.

Before we look at the situation in Ulster today it is worth pausing to reflect on this long and tortuous involvement of the English in Irish affairs—eight hundred years.

One of the English administration during the reign of Queen Elizabeth I was the poet Edmund Spenser—best remembered for the 'Faerie Queene'. On the basis of his experiences in Ireland he posed an intriguing question:

> There have been divers good plots devised, and wise counsels cast already about reformation of that realm; but they say, it is the fatal destiny of that land that no purposes whatsoever are meant for her good...or that Almighty God hath not yet

appointed the time of her reformation, or that he reserveth her
in this unquiet state still for some secret scourge, which shall by
her come into England, it is hard to be known, yet much to be
feared.[5]

Spenser would no doubt be amazed to know that his
question, posed in the first Elizabethan age, is still
unanswered four centuries later in the second Elizabethan
period. For seldom has the Irish threat come home to the
English more powerfully than in our generation. Not only
have hundreds of British soldiers died in the present conflict;
Aire Neave, Conservative Party Spokesman on Northern
Ireland was killed in March 1978 within the precincts of the
Palace of Westminster; just over a year later, Lord Mountbatten, the Duke of Edinburgh's uncle, was killed by a
terrorist bomb. Christians are aware that God is the judge
of all the nations of the earth. That makes it at least a valid
question to ask—was Spenser right when he suggested that
God might bring judgement to England through its connection with Ireland?

This is a question which most will not feel able to answer
one way or the other with any certainty. It is however a
dimension that must be faced. As God is the Lord of history
he is involved, not to say implicated, in what has happened
over these eight hundred years. At the very least we must
seek to understand what he is saying to us today, conscious
of this legacy of the past.

Sean O'Casey, the great Irish playwright, gives us food
for thought on this issue in his play 'Juno and the Paycock'.
The play deals with the civil war that engulfed the Irish
Free State in the first few years of its existence. Mary is
talking to her friend, Mrs Boyle, about the death of her
brother in the street fighting.

'Oh it's thrue, it's thrue what Jerry Devine says—there isn't a

God, there isn't a God; if there was he wouldn't let these things happen!'

Mrs Boyle: 'Mary, you mustn't say them things. We'll want all the help we can get from God and his blessed Mother now! These things have nothing to do with the Will o' God. Ah, what can God do agen the stupidity of men!'

The 'stupidity of men' (and many of them English) has undoubtedly caused this problem, but it also has *something* to do with the will of God!

3. Fightings Without and Fears Within

There is no need to catalogue the events of the present troubles. They have become part of our daily life through the television news bulletins over the past years. This television journalism, good and informative as it generally is, inevitably gives an unbalanced picture. Life is not all bombs and bullets on the one hand, but, on the other, the statistics of murder conceal a depth and extent of human tragedy which is rarely conveyed in the news media.

For most, life has an air of reasonable normality, The extent to which people in Northern Ireland have got used to living with the troubles came home to me a few years ago when I was spending a day in Belfast with a friend who was over from England. It was a day that reflected accurately the TV image of 'bombs on every corner'.

For most of the morning and afternoon there were many army jeeps and saracens with sirens blaring dashing around the city. Armed police were stationed on every corner. From above came the continual drone of the army helicopters. Twice we were stopped with crowds of others as bombs went off just around the corner. The police and army were kept busy cordoning off different parts of the city as the bomb disposal experts investigated hoaxes and detonated others.

It was an inconvenience; it was not possible to get to the

shops you wanted to go to; most of us were caught in traffic jams as we went home because the police had closed off one of the motorways out of the city because of a suspect bomb. But, of all the people I noticed that day (apart from the security forces who were rushing around continually) most were only interrupted briefly in what they were doing.

During the afternoon we went to see a film in a cinema not thirty yards away from the debris of a bomb that had exploded that morning. It was not bravery, bravado, or foolhardiness! It was a small indication of how we as human beings quickly adjust to the inevitable and accept it as normal.

Broadly speaking, the one and a half million inhabitants of Northern Ireland have got used to the situation. The searching when you enter a shop, the police and army road blocks that occur at random, and the sight of armed soldiers and police with guns at the ready, patrolling through shopping centres—all these have become accepted as part of daily life.

It is also true that since the height of the violence of the early seventies life has become more normal (though 1981 and 1982 have seen a significant escalation in tension and renewed killings). Some have even talked of 'an acceptable level of violence'! But with well over two thousand civilians, police and soldiers killed since 1969, and with that figure still growing by more than one killing a week, it is clearly far from acceptable.

Perhaps one of the reasons why some talk of an acceptable level of violence is because of a weariness with the situation, a feeling that nothing can be done. One English observer expressed it graphically to me:

Perhaps it is time to admit failure, time for us to come home. It would be a hard thing to do—to leave them to it. But we may as well be realistic. No solution will be found. We've done the most we can. Now, with the sadness of a detective who writes 'Enquiry Closed' on the documents of an unsolved murder, we should realize that nothing more can be done.

This sense of weariness and hopelessness is under-standable. It has been going on for well over a decade. When the present conflict began, Cunards's new ship QE2 was about to make its maiden voyage; Prince Charles was invested Prince of Wales in Caernarvon Castle; man first walked on the moon and Concorde carried its first passen-gers. It all seems an age ago! But the Christian way is never to give up in the face of deep rooted problems. The servant of God 'will faithfully bring forth justice' (Is 42:3–4).

For those living in Northern Ireland there is no 'giving up'. The emigration rate has been surprisingly low. It is 'home' and the determination to see things through is very strong. But, for those for whom Northern Ireland will never be 'home' it is very difficult to comprehend the feelings of those who belong there—although without some attempt to do so it is very difficult to pray effectively for the situation.

The feel of what it must be like to be a Catholic living in Northern Ireland impressed itself upon me forcefully when I was watching a television programme. It was an ITV documentary which condensed three years of the present conflict into one hour. I was watching this programme with a Christian friend from the Bogside in Derry. I can remember few more painful and embarrassing moments than when we saw the events of Bloody Sunday. We saw again the British Paratroopers firing on demonstrators in Derry. Many were hit in the back; thirteen died. My friend could remember this day and also several other occasions when he was kept awake all night as the army turned their house over—and they were none too gentle! I have walked with this same friend past the impressive stone monument in the Bogside erected, as it proclaims, to the memory of those 'who were murdered by British paratroopers on Bloody Sunday, 30th January, 1972'. Government inquiries have also acknowledged that there have been other proven cases of brutality against Catholics by both the army and Ulster's police force. For those of us who have never experienced the police and the army as those who represent a hostile regime we find it very hard to *feel* what many Catholics in Northern Ireland have undergone over the past years.

Then few of us, seeing the police and army on the receiving end of petrol bombs, can appreciate how *they* feel. I well remember talking with a young British soldier—like many, still in his teens. He had a kind of mental block about service in Northern Ireland. It was something not to talk about; 'best not to acknowledge the feelings and then the pain doesn't hurt.' But he began to talk about going on patrol in Belfast with the constant fear that anyone he met was a potential killer. Soldiers cannot fire first, though going down a dark alley at night and seeing a suspicious figure lurking in the shadows—whose finger would not get itchy on the trigger? When a patrol goes to search an area where one or more of their friends have been killed in an ambush is it surprising that they feel like 'having a go' at those whom they suspect of the murder, or that they get a little rough with those they think are shielding the killers? None of these feelings can ever justify retaliation on the part of the security forces but *their* feelings are also part of the human tragedy, for they are people too. I recall an army padre saying that he was impressed by the high level of restraint shown by the vast majority of soldiers. 'I tremble, sometimes,' he said, 'when I see them go out. Young lads—some of their friends are relaxing at university—but they have one of the most psychologically demanding jobs in the UK. Sometimes they get a bit rough. But then they're only sinners like the rest of us.'

Many in England find it most difficult of all to enter into the feelings of the Ulster Protestant. They are fellow British subjects, loyal to the crown, and Protestants, but the Ulster varieties of both are very different from the English. The histories on TV and elsewhere give them a bad press. They pay dearly for the years of the Unionist ascendancy. Collectively their history is seen to be against them—yet individually they are immensely likeable people who since 1969 have known many personal tragedies. They wonder where it will lead to. They fear that the only solution which English politicians can envisage will mean the end to their province as they know it.

Writing at the end of 1981 the Rev. John Dunlop, a Presbyterian Minister portrayed well the feelings of his community:

> At the present time part of the Protestant reluctance to see significant numbers of Catholics move into a neighbourhood is the suspicion that some of the new residents may be Provisional activists or sympathisers. If they are, then people such as policemen, prison officers, firemen and part-time soldiers are put at risk. Take the recent case of a fireman with a young family who was warned by the police that his name was on the IRA hit list. His wife and he now live under constant strain.... The recent demonstrations in the towns and cities of Northern Ireland after Robert Bradford's murder should be understood, in part, as protests by people who have taken about as much murder as they can stomach. To encourage the politics of co-operation in this environment is to go right against the prevailing trends...the Protestant community has gone through a series of emotional shocks in the last thirteen years. The people feel that they have been unfairly ridiculed and maligned as being a hard-hearted discriminating gang of bigots. It seems that the world has found them guilty. Meanwhile they feel outraged that the Provisional IRA has taken every opportunity to shoot them to pieces and has won the propaganda war at the same time. If a people feel this, it affects their spiritual well-being.[1]

Perhaps the deepest feeling that underlies all others is the ever-present reality of fear. On present indications many people have few real grounds to fear being shot. Unless a person is a member of the security forces (and, of course, several thousand Protestants are part-time members of the Ulster Defence Regiment) or part of a paramilitary group, they do not come under much direct threat of being killed. But that does not eradicate the fear of the possibility. There are sadly the cases of innocent bystanders being killed, and often these are young people. It might be a youth, Catholic or Protestant, who is shot in a revenge killing just because he happened to be standing on a corner, as a motorbike with its shotgun passenger sped by. Others are the victims of bombs meant for other people. An innocent child might be killed by a police vehicle involved in street rioting or by a stray rubber bullet.

Very few talk of such fears, but they are there under the surface. People under twenty can remember very little else. To them the life of tension and fear is the only one they know and they, inevitably, accept it as normal. Mary Grant is a nun who lives in the Falls Road. In one of her meditations she speaks of this fear that is bred in adults by the present tragic situation—children are now born with it.

When I came to live in this city first, my immediate reaction to hesitant queries was, 'Of course I'm not afraid!'

Then one night I dropped a friend in East Belfast, a part of the city I wasn't familiar with: I missed a turn and found myself lost—every tiny street was blocked at the end, every time I turned, my headlights picked up King Billy on the walls, and slogans.

It seemed every door opened to see who was in the strange car. I was seized with nameless terror. I could not get out and ask my way. I felt threatened, trapped, alone.

In that night I realized how the fears of our environment had entered into me, despite myself. I understood the fears of those who walked alone at night, defenceless; I understood the fear of many people who had not left their district in years, never entered the unknown behind the barriers. Some children have never seen behind the barriers their parents have erected.[2]

This kind of fear controls far more than most people in Northern Ireland realize. Most Protestants would not dream of going into the Falls Road or Andersonstown, and likewise most Catholics would never set foot in the Shankill Road or certain parts of East Belfast. It is a fear that restricts our freedom. I know myself feelings of apprehension as I have driven through the Falls and seen an 'Anti-Brit' demonstration or seen a group of teenagers in the Bogside jeering at a patrol of British soldiers. As I see the slogans on the walls that proclaim 'Brits out' or the H-Block posters that shout 'Margaret Thatcher: wanted for murder!' I am aware of very primitive instincts of fear and self-preservation welling up within.

John McKeown is a Catholic who knows well this fear. He has seen it dominate his life and the lives of most of his friends. He is, like most, one of the 'innocent victims' of the troubles. But his is not a depressing story. It is full of encouragement and hope, for it not only shows some of the worst effects of suspicion, fear and hatred. It also reveals that perfect love, the love of God, which casts out fear. It is the other side of the Northern Ireland story—the one you will not see on the television news. But it is the greatest news that comes out of the heart of the Ulster tragedy.

John recalls what it was like in the early seventies.

There was a long run of sectarian killings in Belfast and he remembers how he felt at the time. 'Lots of Protestants and British soldiers were being shot dead. Every time I heard on the news that a man had been killed in Belfast I listened for his name and where he lived. If it turned out to be 'one of them', then really and truly I used to jump for joy.

In fact, many a time I could have gone out and shot one of them myself; I was filled with so much hatred.'

Yet John had not been brought up with that degree of hatred for Protestants and the British. He has never been involved in any paramilitary organization but, through the early part of the present troubles, his family suffered so much harassment that a fierce hatred took hold of him and grew like a cancer within him.

Like nearly all Roman Catholics in Northern Ireland he had been to a Catholic School and, of course, all Protestants go to their own schools. 'I was brought up in the Ardoyne in the tradition that Protestants are boys to throw stones at. We were always on our side of the divide. I didn't hate them at the time—it was just them and us. It's always been like that.'

It was not only the education system that emphasized the difference. He noticed it more when he tried to get his first job. When prospective employers heard that he went to the Sacred Heart School, all of a sudden there was no job. The feeling of 'them and us' deepened, but still there was no hatred. It was accepted by so many as an inevitable part of life under the Unionist Ascendancy.

Like many Catholics, John won through in spite of the system. He landed a good job in the construction industry and, although he met some abuse from Protestant work-mates, he soon rose to the position of foreman.

By 1968, he had been married to Margaret for some years and already had four children: they were at the stage when they needed to move from their small home. They bought a larger one on the Protestant side of the Crumlin Road in Belfast. This was still an acceptable thing to do for the troubles were, as yet, a few months away. They felt secure and settled for life. They had worked hard and put all they had into the new house. There they would raise the family, which would, no doubt, grow a little more, and they would see them off to a good start in life.

A few months later the troubles began. Soon it was made clear that many Protestants objected to having Catholics on their patch. The police had to guard the area each night. It was less pleasant than it had been in those first few months but perhaps, people hoped, things would soon settle down again.

It was not to be. One Friday in 1969 John was called home from work to discover that two men had been around and told the family that they must be gone by that evening or be burnt out. Understandably, his wife was terrified. But the army and police promised protection, and for three nights there were two men guarding the street. All remained quiet. On the fourth day the patrol was taken off. That same night every Catholic in the street was put out, evicted by a Protestant Paramilitary leader who was backed by a menacing looking mob of five or six hundred. Fortunately John had taken his family out for a run in the car and missed the actual eviction itself. As they had no chance of getting back into their home they stayed with a relative for the night. The next day they were given a council house in Antrim, twenty miles to the north.

After a few weeks the army and the parish priest thought that things had calmed down sufficiently for them to return. John wanted to make the attempt, but he was not sure how his wife would feel for she was suffering very badly with nervous trouble as a result of the harassment of the past weeks. The house itself was now a somewhat forbidding place—its front windows were boarded up against the rioting. But it was still their home, and John persuaded Margaret to move back with their four children. They were hoping, almost against hope, that it would work out alright this time.

Christmas was drawing near. It was a good time to hope for a more peaceful period. Perhaps, in the season of goodwill there would be a sufficient lull in the troubles for normal life to win through. But just twelve days before Christmas, any such thoughts were shattered. A bomb was thrown at the back of the house and all the windows were blown out.

If they left again they knew they would never return. They had to stay in their own house, if at all possible. And they managed it, though the situation was often very menacing. Then followed the court proceedings to obtain compensation for the bombing of their home. They were awarded a mere pittance—£25. Their anger at what they saw as gross injustice on the part of the police and the courts was understandable. The thought, always there in Northern Ireland, that it is only Protestants that get a fair deal inevitably deepened.

Consequently, John's anger was directed, not so much at the officers of the system—the police and army, but at those behind it—the Protestant people of Ulster. He felt a hatred for the majority community burning deeper into his soul. He made no allowances—'Anybody who was a Protestant was no good.' These feelings made no distinction between good and bad Protestants. He could not understand that the same was happening to some Protestants in predominantly Catholic areas. He could not acknowledge that there were Protestants who would feel real concern for him and for the plight of his family. He never met such individuals. He met them all in the guise of an unfriendly system and the mobs in the streets. This is the tragedy for both communities: once a society has become 'ghetto-ized' as is so with much of Ulster, then the other community ceases to be an assortment of individuals, good and bad; rather it is a hostile system. Bridges of friendship, compassion and understanding can only be built between people, and such personal contact is normally not possible between the ghettos. John, as so many others in both communities, was caught in the trap of a ghetto-dominated society which so easily breeds suspicion, fear and hatred.

The following June the family were again put out by a threatening mob. It was the last straw—they knew that they could not return. Their furniture was put into a warehouse in the dock area but subsequently moved by the authorities into a store in the Shankill Road (staunch Protestant territory). As John recalls, 'They might just as well have left it in the street and written on it 'this belongs to a Fenian' because a gang just took sledge hammers to it and smashed the lot.' This time, there was no compensation at all.

For the rest of the year they lived in the refuge chalets on the Glen Road. Margaret's health continued to deteriorate. Her asthma became so bad that she nearly died. John's feelings were inevitable. 'If it hadn't been for those Protestants doing these things she wouldn't be in the state she's in now.'

At the beginning of 1970 they moved out into a house in Andersonstown, one of the Catholic estates in West Belfast—they have lived there ever since. It was the time of sectarian killings, no-go areas, house-searches by the army and internment without trial. John can remember being hauled in for questioning by the army. It was a bitter experience. The innocent as well as the guilty felt they were being treated as criminals. 'We were taken to the local school,' John recalls, 'and were stamped like cattle by the army to show we had been taken in already for questioning. Many were dragged out of their homes—some were beaten up. And all the time the hatred was growing in me more and more. I saw soldiers getting shot and I was glad.

John had never been a committed Christian He describes himself as having been a half-hour a week Catholic who went to mass on Sunday but thought nothing more of his faith for the rest of the week. It was a faith that could not survive the pressures of the troubles. 'It got that I no longer could believe in God. I still went to Mass, but it was only for the sake of Margaret and the children.' It was the same for many, both Catholic and Protestant. Religion was for many just a part of their community identity rather than a living faith in a God who could do anything about what was happening.

It was through Margaret that things began to change. With a priest-friend she went to one of the early charismatic meetings in Northern Ireland. John drove them there. He did not go in though: the very thought of it did his state of mind no good at all, for some at the meeting were Protestants! But that evening saw the beginning of a great transformation in Margaret's life. She met the Lord in a deeply personal way and was baptized in the Holy Spirit. But John was far from impressed. 'Margaret came home,' he remembers, 'speaking in tongues. That didn't go down very well with me. She was sick enough in the head before she went. She had come home quite mad!'

In spite of his coolness Margaret persevered. Every week she would go to the prayer meeting which had just started in Andersonstown. It was proving a great help to her but John had increasing difficulties with it as more Protestants were beginning to attend. For them it was a big step to take and it showed the miracle of the transforming love of God in both Catholic and Protestant that was making this possible. To John it seemed very different—he knew nothing of God's love for Protestants, only the deep hatred burning away inside him. He remembers how he sat outside in the car waiting for Margaret to come out and all the time inwardly cursing the Protestants who were in the meeting.

There was something new growing in Margaret's life, and clearly God was also healing her. John was being affected though he hardly realized it. The Spirit of God was moving into those deep places of hatred and blindness and one Wednesday—for no particular reason that John understood—he went with Margaret to the prayer meeting. It proved to be a very confusing experience. What most sticks in his mind from that first meeting was the number of his fellow Roman Catholics who kept reading from the Bible. 'I was brought up just as an ordinary traditional Catholic. I never read a Bible. I remember we used to go down to the Customs House in Belfast and jeer at the Bible-thumpers. That's all I knew of the Bible—that it was something used by these strange people. I didn't even know what the Bible was. Now these fellows in the charismatic meeting were all quoting from the Bible—to me, that made them Protestants.'

He continued to go, though his confusion only deepened. Often people would share 'words from the Lord' or 'a prophecy' and he had no idea what all that was about. Then at one meeting someone gave a prophecy, part of which hit him between the eyes—'My son, I want you to put your trust in me.' John knew that God was speaking directly to him—and he yelled out at the top of his voice, 'But I do trust you, Lord.'

It was a first impulsive step. Ever since that day John has been eager to attend the meetings—to learn and to grow in his new-found relationship with the Lord. 'I remember soon after that time reading from Psalm 34, 'This poor man cried and the Lord heard him.' That was what happened to me. Ever since then I've been a changed man. My faith has become real. Now, when I go to Mass, I really meet with Jesus—before I just went because it looked right. People used to say that the Son of God died for me on the cross and I would think, 'Well, that's way back there—nothing to do with me.' Now I know that it's true. I know that it was for me personally that Jesus died.'

In the first year of his new-found life there was so much for John to discover. Most of all he found that, through the baptism of God's Spirit and the infilling of his love, he now had a deep love for Protestants. The old hatred had been removed. It was a profound healing that could only come about through the work of God's Spirit.

Some time later he was asked to give his testimony before six and a half thousand people at the National Charismatic Conference in Dublin. Afterwards the Rev. Cecil Kerr, who had been a speaker at the Conference, came up to him and asked forgiveness for all the hurt that he and his people had caused John and his family. They embraced one another and ever since then Cecil, a Protestant minister, has been a major influence, under God, in John's life. In a series of seminars many years later in his own Parish church, John was asked, 'What great person in your life has made you a better Catholic?' He had no doubts. The first name he wrote down was Cecil Kerr. That sounds an almost crazy statement to make in the context of Northern Ireland. It shows the miraculous dimension of the work of God's Spirit.

As John looks back on the past ten years since he has come to know the Lord he concludes, 'I can now stop and talk to the army and the police. I can speak to them as brothers. All I feel for them is love. I only wish I could do more to express that, but you have to be very careful in the situation as it is in West Belfast.

'I now praise God for all that has happened to me—even for being put out of my house. I cursed God at the time because I did not understand what was going on. I believe he could have stopped it if he had wanted. But he allowed it to happen, and I praise him for it. Without it all I wouldn't be where I am today. God has done so much for me and my family.'

John is one of the many signs of what God can do in people's lives—and a lot of people, including soldiers, have noticed the difference and been affected deeply by it. John and Margaret keep open house in the middle of Andersonstown for anyone. And many an evening there are Protestants there sharing their life and praying together.

John has also seen hundreds of Catholic people in West Belfast and elsewhere changed by God through charismatic renewal and he is clear about what is the heart of the trouble. 'The reason I jumped for joy when Protestants were killed was because I had let Satan take control. He has done that with an awful lot of people who throw stones and bombs and shout at the police and the army. They need release from Satan—and the only way is by prayer in the name of Jesus. We need to pray that God will change other people's lives like he's changed mine.'

4. Is It a Religious War?

> In Ireland there are two acceptable reactions to a crisis. The first is to get down on your knees and pray to God. The second is to go down on one knee, lift a gun and try to shoot the head off your opponent.

Rosita Sweetman's statement[1] is far from true—but it is how many people around the world see it. They think that the conflict is between two opposing groups of Christians who are shooting it out to win supremacy for their particular religious tradition.

In reaction to this erroneous and simplistic view many have wanted to emphasize that the troubles are not a religious conflict at all. For example, in 1981 readers of the *Church of England Newspaper* were assured that 'the division is a nationalist one with social and racial overtones...it is, however, in no sense a religious conflict'.[2] It is a relief for Christians to be told that—it assures us that we are not to blame. But is it true?

The truth of the situation is manifestly more complex than a fight for Protestant views of doctrine and spirituality over against those of the Roman Catholic Church—or vice-versa. But to say that it is 'in no sense a religious conflict' can be a way of avoiding one of the major questions that the churches must face. To what extent is Christianity involved or implicated in the present struggle? Are there some who are deliberately involved in the conflict because they are fighting for their particular understanding of the gospel? Are there those who justify their actions in the name of Christ? Are the churches called into question by their seeming inability or unwillingness to follow through the radical demands of the gospel and thus become a spearhead in the solution of the problem?

These are hard questions to ask, but they cannot be avoided. I have several times heard people in different parts of the world say that they have rejected Christianity because of what they see as evidence in Northern Ireland of its ineffectiveness, even its harmfulness. Have Ulster and its churches become 'a byword among the nations?' It is important to realize that these hard questions are asked of the churches throughout the whole of the British Isles, for by past and present involvement the combined witness of the church in these islands is implicated.

From the perspective of an American observer, a Christian journalist puts his finger on the central nerve of this issue. 'Christians, of course, find it hard to admit that that which is so central in their lives—their faith—can be a factor in a shameful scandal such as that in Northern Ireland. No doubt faith is not to blame. But that which has passed for religion in Ireland...has certainly been, and remains today, a large part of the problem.'[3]

When Pope John Paul II visited Ireland he was at pains to free the churches from any implication in the present conflict.

The tragic events taking place in Northern Ireland do not have their source in the fact of belonging to different churches and Confessions; that this is not—despite what is so often repeated before world opinion—a religious war, a struggle between Catholics and Protestants. On the contrary, Catholics and

Protestants, as people who confess Christ, taking inspiration from their faith in the gospel, are seeking to draw closer to one another in unity and peace. When they recall the greatest commandment of Christ, the commandmant of love, they cannot behave otherwise.

Sadly this is true *only* as the confident Christian hope of what *will* be for it is far ahead of what *is*. While there is much evidence that many are seeking to live openly in love and unity with their Protestant or Catholic brethren, the majority still find this idea religiously unacceptable.

From his perspective as an Irish Catholic priest, Father Enda McDonagh, Professor of Moral Theology at Maynooth, addresses himself to the central issue of the involvement and indictment of the church within the present conflict. 'Is Northern Ireland, with its continuing violence and deep seated religious division, a symbol of the final failure of our conventional church allegiances and their halting Christianity?'[4]

In our glance at the history behind the present conflict we have seen that, while church allegiance is not the only factor, it is one of them—alongside a complex mixture of cultural, linguistic, social, economic and political factors. Until the time of the Protestant Reformation, religious differences were not part of the struggle. It was a straight-forward matter of who was the dominant political power in Ireland. This political dimension has continued as one of the major roots of the conflict in the last four hundred years and this factor in itself has been complicated by the coming of other parties to the conflict who have been equally concerned to gain political power for themselves. But, since the Reformation, the religious dimension has increasingly taken its place alongside the other factors.

In essence, until 1921, the religious conflict had been the attempt to replace Roman Catholicism with Protestantism.

Different tactics had been used to achieve this end—through legal declaration and ecclesiastical imposition in the Tudor and Stuart periods; through the expressly religious militarism of the Puritan campaign under Oliver Cromwell; by erosion through the Penal law against Roman Catholics in the eighteenth and early nineteenth centuries; and, from the mid-nineteenth to early twentieth centuries, through aggressive anti-Roman Catholic evangelism as represented at the time by such movements as the Irish Church Missions. In the event, all of these failed to loosen the hold of Roman Catholicism on the majority of the Irish population—in fact they probably account, in large measure, for its continued strength.

These fundamentally religious elements are part of the historical consciousness that continues to fuel this conflict. In themselves these particular religious motivations have been evident in various guises in different ages and in different groups of people. In the present conflict it is possible, by way of example, to isolate two clear manifestations of such religious motivation—one Catholic, the other Protestant.

In neither case do I want to suggest that the religious factor has become the dominant motivation within that community; the main sources of the conflict are clearly nationalist/republican aspirations on the one hand, and Unionist/Separatist defence on the other. But for some, these religious factors have become very powerful indeed. We consider first the more obvious of the two—the Protestant.

1. Fighting for the gospel

Since the separation of the six northern counties into a 'Protestant State' distinct from the twenty-six counties of the Free State, the religious motivation of Protestantism has become far more one of defence and maintenance than of expansion and proselytism. And the present conflict bears eloquent testimony to a powerful religious motivation at least in a significant section of Protestantism, namely the more 'anti-Roman Catholic fundamentalist' groupings.[5] These may be in the minority among Protestants in general, but they are a potent force nevertheless. They are committed to the crusade for Protestant Truth over against Roman Catholicism as a central issue in the present conflict.

Two Methodist leaders, who because of their contacts across the divide have been labelled 'strange gods' and 'fickle' by Ian Paisley, acknowledge the force that Paisley has become. 'Large and strong physically, he bestrides the religio-political scene like a Colossus. His energy and considerable ability to sway crowds with his oratory make him a force to be reckoned with. Yet he was laughed at and dismissed by church leaders and politicians in his early days as an incongruous and irrelevant figure.'[6]

Many non-Ulstermen also find Paisley difficult to understand because of the particular brand of extreme Northern Ireland Presbyterian fundamentalism that he represents— it is foreign to them. This is demonstrated in an amusing encounter between Ian Paisley and James Callaghan when the latter was Home Secretary. The conversation between the two of them had been difficult. Searching for a sentiment on which they could both agree without hesitation Mr Callaghan said, 'You know, Mr Paisley, we are all children of God.' Like lightning came the damning reply, 'No, we are not, Mr Callaghan. We are all children of wrath.' Had Callaghan desired to continue the argument, which I doubt would have been advisable, he could have turned to Paul's address to the Athenians in Acts chapter 17 where Paul reminds his hearers that we are all 'God's offspring' by virtue of our creation. But Ian Paisley's riposte went straight to the heart of his gospel—the concern to emphasize judgement. He was, of course, right—we are all children of wrath, but his rebuke to Callaghan highlights the general flavour of his whole approach to Christianity. Judgement and negativeness are so emphasized that they seem to dominate all else. Love gets very scant mention; at times it is equated with 'wishy-washy' liberal ideas. The concern is to define Christianity in terms of what we are not; it has an inbuilt tendency to exclude others, and the only way to be included is to adopt in every detail its particular doctrinal, social and political attitudes.

It is this peculiar, essentially negative brand of Christianity that is central to all Ian Paisley aims to achieve, and he himself makes no secret of what is the heart of his success. 'My involvement politically is because of my involvement spiritually. People don't seem to realize it but this is a religious battle which has been fought on the political plane and the problem is not an economic problem.'[7]

Many outside of Northern Ireland find it difficult to believe this claim that he makes about himself—that, first and foremost, he is a preacher of the gospel. But, given his own particular sectarian and narrow understanding of the gospel, the facts seem to bear him out.

Some years ago I was showing two visiting English clergymen around Northern Ireland. As part of 'the tour' we went to hear Dr Paisley preach. We arrived at his church in the Ravenhill Road in Belfast just before 7.00 p.m. on Sunday evening. We were greeted at the church door by one of the elders and shown to our seats in the gallery. There were well over a thousand in the congregation.

It is a very pleasant modern church known as 'Martyrs' Memorial'. It is the 'cathedral' of the Free Presbyterian Church of which Dr Paisley is the Moderator, a position he has held since founding the denomination in 1951.

I had been to the church several times before and so I

knew what to expect—a typical kind of non-conformist service with lengthy extempore prayer, hearty singing and a very compelling sermon. All is presided over by the dominant figure of Ian Paisley in frock coat.

For my two friends it was their first live encounter with 'Paisleyism'; they were not sure what to expect. They knew the Ian Paisley of the TV interview—the very forceful politician who seemed to terrify most interviewers whose unhappy lot it was to have to tackle him. Like most Englishmen they imagined him to be first and foremost a politician. They were no doubt bewildered by his style 'Rev.'. They may have assumed that this was simply a hangover from a former profession. In common with many others they certainly felt that his belligerent and sectarian attitudes were far from Christian.

Our visit to his church deeply challenged this secular television image of Ian Paisley. On that evening he preached for forty-five minutes on 'How can we be sure that the Bible is the word of God?' It was gripping. I, and no doubt many others, could have listened for much longer. It was powerfully delivered and, although I found his argument spurious on one or two points, his presentation was utterly convincing. I doubt that many would have left the church that evening without being thoroughly persuaded of the absolute authority, inspiration, infallibility and glory of the word of God—especially as it is translated in the Authorized Version!

He made it abundantly clear that he knows that man's greatest need is to repent and believe the gospel—and that the central passion of his life is to preserve the great truths of God's free grace to undeserving sinners.

The link between his calling as an evangelist and preacher and his commitment to militant 'Unionist' politics is made by certain logical steps. Central to his understanding of the preaching ministry is the need to preserve the truth of the gospel against error—a commitment that we see also in St Paul, particularly in his letter to the Galatians. For Dr Paisley this means a particularly strong stand on two fronts. On the one hand he is a staunch opponent of all liberal and ecumenical theology; on the other hand he is militantly opposed to Roman Catholicism, root and branch.

He believes that the Pope is the anti-Christ and that the Roman Catholic Church is committed to a worldwide campaign to undermine the truths of Protestantism. He sees the very existence of the gospel of free grace to be the issue at stake. The Church of Rome is 'the scarlet whore' and all kinds of tactics are to be expected from her. It follows that the reunification of Ireland would be foolish. The gospel truth would be swallowed up by the 'papist state'. To his mind every biblical Protestant should be able to see what he understands to be the inescapable logic of a biblical position.

Any Protestant who fails to see the danger in the way he expounds it is branded as a traitor. Thus, when Archbishop Michael Ramsey visited the Pope in 1966, Ian Paisley wrote a stinging article in his church magazine.

> The Archbishop is a traitor—a traitor to the Constitution—and I charge him and indict him of high treason against this realm. The Pope said to Dr Ramsey that he was glad that the bridge which had been broken down between Rome and England he (the Archbishop) had repaired. By the grace of God we will place the dynamite of Protestant Truth under his reconstructed bridge and blow it to smithereens. The Archbishop is like Terence O'Neill—he is a modern bridge builder: a bridge and a traitor are alike in one thing—they both take you to the other side. In this day of crisis both O'Neill and Ramsey would like to take us to the other side.[8]

Captain O'Neill, the then Northern Ireland premier, is placed alongside Michael Ramsey as a traitor because, in 1965, he initiated an exchange visit with Sean Lemass, Prime Minister of the Irish Republic. For Ian Paisley the threat in such a meeting was the religious one of Roman Catholicism taking over and obliterating the gospel truths of Protestantism.

Paisley speaks often of the conspiracy among leaders, both in church and state, who are seeking to bring the nation under Roman bondage. He saw the visit of the Pope to Britain in June 1982 as part of a Jesuit plot, of which he often speaks, to undermine the Protestant monarchy and constitution of the United Kingdom. When asked about the meeting at Buckingham Palace, between the Pope and the Queen, he issued the dire warning, 'Whom the Pope blesses, God curses. History is full of examples that show the truth of this.' And many people in Northern Ireland believe what he says, for he and his colleagues are expert communicators, as is seen in the following 'retranslation' of a famous hymn which first appeared in *The Protestant Telegraph*.

> Onward Christian Soldiers
>   Marching unto Rome
> Where a smiling Pontiff
>   Bids us 'welcome home'.
> Our enchanted 'Bishops'
>   Lead the steady flow,
> Forward to St Peter's
>   See their banners go.
>
> Methodists may perish,
>   Wesley call in vain.
> Martin Luther's doctrine
>   Is surely on the wane.
> Cranmer, Ridley, Latimer,

> Let them all 'get lost',
> On! to Lourdes and Fatima
> Counting not the cost.

His appeal is widespread. The Free Presbyterian Church is said to be the fastest growing church in Northern Ireland. It nearly always grows at the expense of other churches who lose their members; people who feel that it is Ian Paisley who *really* understands the heart of the matter, and that there is no one else who will be quite as reliable when the crunch comes.

It is this dominance as a religious leader that has led to his dominance as a political leader. In 1970 he won seats both in Stormont and at Westminster. At the moment he sits as an M.P. in both the United Kingdom and the European Parliaments, as well as leading his party in the Stormont Assembly. On many occasions he has shown that, if necessary, his campaign will be supported by force. He has led demonstrations that official reports have later condemned as violent; he himself has been imprisoned for disorderly conduct and refusing to keep the peace; he has assembled on hillsides at the dead of night with several hundred men, waving firearm certificates, and at the end of 1981 he called into being the militant Third Force.

He has a large following, far larger than the membership of his own church, and he thrives most when the situation is particularly polarized as it was during the Hunger Strike in 1981. At this time he made monumental gains in the local government elections. His own party, the Democratic Unionists, gained nearly as many seats, province-wide, as the Official Unionists.

While not all his followers hold to the religious views that lead to his particular brand of politics, there is a large core of support that is wholeheartedly committed, as he is himself, to the religious struggle which they believe to be at the very heart of the conflict.

It is a religious basis which needs to be challenged vigorously—though graciously! The logic of its argument seems convincing at first glance and it is communicated very persuasively. But it does not stand in the light of the good news of Jesus as we see this in the New Testament. There is nothing in the message of Jesus—or for that matter in the position of the present Pope—that allows us to describe the Pope as 'the antichrist' or the church that he leads as the 'scarlet whore'. At best these are mere fatuitous and totally indefensible equations—there must be many others in the world today far more qualified to be dubbed 'antichrist'. At worst the people who thus describe the Pope are foolishly ignoring the warning that Jesus gave, 'Judge not, that you be not judged. For with the judgment you pronounce you will be judged, and the measure you give will be the measure you get' (Mt 7:1–2). Far from seeing the Roman Catholic Church as irredeemably apostate and abandoned by God there is ample evidence in our time (far more than in many others) to show that God's Spirit is moving within that Church at all levels and in countless different ways. The problem with bigoted sectarianism is that it refuses to countenance the evidence that is plain for all to see.

Also the love and passion of Jesus, and his desire for the unity of his church which he expressed in his high priestly prayer on the night before he died, both point to the need for us all to affirm our unity with Roman Catholic Christians as one within the body of Christ. It is this commitment to reconciliation with all its pain and suffering, as well as its glory, that expresses the way of Christ, and not the militant Protestant defence, by all manner of means, of its own politically-fortified supremacy. 'I submit' rather than 'No Surrender' was the mark of Jesus' commitment in the Garden of Gethsemane—'no guile was found on his lips.

When he was reviled he did not revile in return; when he suffered, he did not threaten; but he trusted to him who judges justly' (1 Pet 2:22–23).

The gospel of free grace to undeserving sinners, the gospel of salvation which is received by faith through grace alone—this is indeed God's truth, and there are occasions on which it is necessary firmly to defend its integrity. But there are ways of defending it—such as some that Ian Paisley and his followers employ—which in themselves constitute a denial of that very gospel of love and reconciliation which we see in Jesus. Much of what happens in Northern Ireland is motivated by such a Paisley version of the gospel. It is a dangerous perversion, and only a Christlike demonstration of the biblical gospel will expose the false.

There are many Protestants who see the flaws in Ian Paisley's version of the gospel, and they sometimes find it difficult not to hit back in anger for the sectarian division that he continues to inflame. But clearly that cannot be the way. It is when the love and truth of Jesus are demonstrated and proclaimed that the harsh distortion will be seen for what it is. Furthermore, it is important that Christians make clear that in no way is the good news of Jesus a justification for the sectarian struggle that is going on; rather, the gospel stands in judgement upon it.

2. A martyr theology

The specifically religious motivation that has been evident among some within the Roman Catholic community is of a very different kind. It is the notion of Christ's sacrifice being re-enacted in the nationalist struggle. It is a very powerful and compelling idea, often eloquently expressed, but it also must be challenged as a distortion of the gospel.

This belief was visually promoted in the H-block posters

which were displayed on walls all over Ireland in support of those on hunger strike in both 1980 and 1981. One poster in particular was of a young man with long black hair—he had a sad expression on his face with eyes that cried out for pity. Down his face there streamed what looked like blood. Many noticed the implicit message. Here were young men passively giving their life-blood for Ireland; they were a new generation of martyrs.

Not all republicans saw it this way, perhaps it was only the minority who *consciously* accepted it, but it gave for many a general aura of religious fervour to the whole campaign. Father Denis Faul made the point explicitly:

> It is strange how Irish Catholics instinctively come back to the Mass—that was the reaction to the announcement of the impending hunger strike in Long Kesh. Centuries of practice, of meditation, of endurance, of choice, lead them to suffering and death as the price of freedom and redemption. Padraig Pearse saw this and phrased it in 1916—Easter Death and Resurrection. The ultimate protest of hunger strike against an unjust system and tyrannical oppression and bigotry ought not to be too unexpected of a country too small and helpless to throw out the centuries-old oppressor who bribes and divides and tortures and covers up with pharisaic respectability…. Sad, but who that aspires to be Christian, will not admit that the protest of suffering and rejection as a sign of moral strength is better than violence against others. Christ died himself alone; he offered his own life, not the lives of others to achieve redemption. No man has a right to call upon others to die violently. He can lead men by the voluntary sacrifice of his own life. By suffering and death endured, moral power is created; by suffering and death inflicted on others immoral evil enters the world—better for Irishmen to select the first option and reject the second.[9]

Father Faul's reference to Padraig Pearse points to the

great exponent of this view of sacrifice for Ireland. He was one of the leaders in the Easter Rising of 1916 who was executed by the British for his part in thàt rebellion. Through his considerable gifts as writer and poet he had forged this link between the nationalist struggle and the very heart of the Christian faith, the sacrifice of Jesus on the cross. In 1913, speaking of Irish freedom, he wrote:

> I do not know if the Messiah has yet come, and I am not sure that there will be any visible and personal Messiah in this redemption: the people itself will perhaps be its own Messiah, the people labouring, scourged, crowned with thorns, agonizing and dying, to rise again immortal and impassable.[10]

The references to the crucifixion are unmistakable.

For Padraig Pearse, Christianity and nationalism were almost one and the same thing—at least they were different sides of the same coin:

> Like a divine religion national freedom bears the works of unity, of sanctity, of catholicity, of apostolic succession. Of unity, for it contemplates the nation as one; of sanctity, for it is holy in itself and in those who serve it; of catholicity, for it embraces all the men and women of the nation; of apostolic succession, for it, or the aspiration after it, passes down from generation to generation from the nation's fathers.[11]

Padraig Pearse saw the nationalist struggle as part of Christ's victory, and it would inevitably mean crucifixion as well as resurrection:

> Ireland will not find Christ's peace until she has taken Christ's sword. What peace she has known these latter days has been the devil's peace, peace with sin, peace with dishonour... Christ's peace is lovely in its coming, beautiful are its feet on the mountains. But it is heralded by terrific messengers; seraphim and cherubim blow trumpets of war before it. We must not

flinch when we are passing through that uproad; we must not faint at the sight of blood. Winning through it, we (or those of us who survive) shall come unto great joy.[12]

In this fight for 'Christ's peace' many would be offering their lives. Pearse and his brother accepted this for themselves as he expressed in the words he put into his mother's mouth in his poem entitled *The Mother*.

> I do not grudge them; Lord, I do not grudge
> My two strong sons that I have seen go out
> To break themselves and die, they and a few,
> In bloody protest for a glorious thing.

Much in these views is reflected in the various theologies of liberation which have emerged during the second half of this century. Pearse's theology foreshadows the later ideas of Christ's liberation being worked out in the political struggles for freedom and human dignity. Those who see liberation theology as a valid interpretation of the biblical gospel will find much to attract them in Pearse's writings.

On the whole the Catholic Church in Ireland—like the Pope himself—seems very wary about liberation theology. There are, however, two issues involved in Pearse's idea of the shedding of blood in the cause of national freedom which relate to the present troubles. First, the shedding of other people's blood, either that of your opponents or that of a comrade whom you order into combat, and secondly voluntary self-sacrifice. In general terms there has been very little theological support in the present conflict for the shedding of other people's blood as a Christian way of attaining a united Ireland. As we have seen, the second idea of offering yourself as a sacrifice for the cause has obtained some theological backing.

Father Faul, in the extract already quoted, denounces as

un-Christian, violence that is used against others. The Roman Catholic Church have held to that view throughout the present struggles. Though at times, to Protestants, they have seemed somewhat slow, the heirarchy have become increasingly unequivocal in their condemnation of violence. Towards the end of 1981, Bishop Philbin, the Bishop of Down and Connor (i.e. Belfast and the surrounding counties of Down and Antrim) said, after the murder of a policeman,

> It is almost certain this murder was planned and carried out by Catholics. It is my duty to declare to them that unless they repent and repudiate this heinous sin they will incur the eternal punishment that God has ordained for what they have done. Those who support their action must know that they share in this guilt.

It is a stand to which the Pope gave his firm backing when speaking at Drogheda on the 29th September 1979.

> Now I wish to speak to all men and women engaged in violence. I appeal to you, in language of passionate pleading. On my knees I beg you to turn away from the paths of violence and return to the ways of peace. You may claim to seek justice. I, too, believe in justice and seek justice. But violence only delays the day of justice. Violence destroys the work of justice. Further violence in Ireland will only drag down to ruin the land you claim to love and the values you claim to cherish. In the name of God I beg you: return to Christ, who died so that men might live in forgiveness and peace. He is waiting for you, longing for each one of you to come to him so that he may say to each of you: your sins are forgiven; go in peace.

It would seem that the majority of practising Roman Catholics agree with the Pope. This was clearly demonstrated when Father Mulvey, a parish priest in Strabane, declared from his pulpit that all violence is wrong and that those who support such men, *even by their silence* are sharing in their guilt. Such views are only infrequently expressed so forthrightly and publicly, but his congregation were delighted. Fifteen hundred of them arranged a meeting in church on the same afternoon to applaud the stand that had been taken by their parish priest.

In relation to the second kind of shedding of blood—self-sacrifice—the reaction has been more equivocal. As we have seen, Father Faul expounded this position with evident passion. There are undeniably echoes within it of the teaching of Jesus—'Greater love has no man than this, that a man lays down his life for his friends' (Jn 15:13). But, in essence, there is an enormous difference between dying for your confession of faith in Jesus (that is the New Testament understanding of martyrdom) and committing suicide for a nationalist cause, however justified that cause may be. This, in the end, was the judgement of the Roman Catholic Church towards the Hunger Strike in the Maze Prison. It was a judgement that many felt was a long time in coming—but, to be fair, most Roman Catholics were, for several weeks, more immediately concerned about what they saw as the inhumane intransigence of the British Government. After some time, the Pope himself sent his personal envoy to persuade the prisoners to abandon their fast. John Paul II is the first to venerate a true martyr, but he obviously saw the hunger strike in an entirely different light.

These are two examples, one Protestant and one Roman Catholic, of how distortions of the gospel are used to give theological and religious justification to various aspects of the present conflict. It is important that all such religious justifications for sectarian strife are seen for what they are—perversions of the good news of Jesus. Then we are free to see that the gospel does indeed have a central place within the conflict. But its place is not to support one side against the other—rather the gospel stands in judgement over our sectarian and denominational divisions and offers a way of making peace.

5. A Risk Worth Taking

I am not ashamed of the gospel: it is the power of God for salvation to everyone who has faith, to the Jew first and also to the Greek' [Rom 1:16].

There is neither Jew nor Greek, there is neither slave nor free, there is neither male nor female; for you are all one in Christ Jesus [Gal 3:28].

The gospel is powerful to change people's lives—to change the very basic attitudes and divisions within society. But it must be the whole gospel of salvation offered freely and without distinction to both Jew and Gentile, or we will not see the whole power. It is this issue that Paul saw so clearly; it was at the heart of his dispute with Peter and the other apostles.

But when Cephas came to Antioch I opposed him to his face, because he stood condemned. For before certain men came from James, he ate with the Gentiles; but when they came he drew back and separated himself, fearing the circumcision party. And with him the rest of the Jews acted insincerely, so that even Barnabas was carried away by their insincerity. [Gal 2:11–13].

A partial gospel, 'for the Jews only' is not the gospel. Gentiles would for ever be second class citizens. It becomes a gospel without power to change one of society's basic problems. It is similar in Ireland today. Traditionally, for many Protestants the position has been, 'No Roman Catholic can be a Christian—they must become a Protestant.' This is the free gospel plus another condition. It is similar to the Jews saying to the Gentiles, 'free salvation plus circumcision'.

I can think of several occasions in Northern Ireland when I've been asked to 'Preach the gospel', or to speak about spiritual renewal but to keep quiet about being part of a Christian community that includes Roman Catholic Christians. It is a seemingly logical request to make in many situations. The argument goes like this: most people here, including many 'born-again' Christians, are too sensitive on the question of Roman Catholics for you to get a hearing if your Catholic links are known. But if we accept those shackles then the gospel loses much of its power; we are bowing to an inadequate gospel and consequently the results will not effect that deep change of heart so needed to cut through the sectarian barrier. What is required is more and more to challenge this desire to preach without mentioning the fulness of the gospel message of reconciliation. It is a risk. It can lead to fierce opposition. But it is only when the whole gospel is preached that we see it working in its full power as that which saves both Jew and Greek, both Catholic and Protestant—and makes us both one in Christ.

The temptation of every preacher, whatever his Society, is to accommodate the gospel to the life-style of those who are already church members. In the western world in general it means often that evangelists omit the challenge to materialism—we feel that western man will not see the news as 'good' if his attitudes to wealth are challenged. We keep quiet not only because the world would object but because the protesting Christian also does not like it.

Speaking of the evangelistic message Jim Wallis concludes rightly that:

> We are called to respond to God always *in the particulars of* our own personal, social and political circumstances....As such, conversion will be a scandal to accepted wisdoms, status quos, and oppressive arrangements. Looking back at biblical and saintly conversions, they can appear romantic. But in the present, conversion is more than a promise of all that might be; it is also a threat to all that is. To the guardian of the social order, genuine biblical conversion will seem dangerous....There are no neutral zones or areas left untouched by biblical conversion.[1]

Reconciliation between Protestant and Catholic in Northern Ireland cannot be treated as a 'neutral zone'. It is not possible to preach the gospel of salvation in the fulness of its power unless this is given its rightful place at the very heart of the proclamation.

We are forced, at this point, to look at the role of the clergy in Northern Ireland, and at the message that moulds their own life-style and governs their preaching. This would be true in any society, for clergy are those who are called, among other things, to teach and to preach. They are ultimately responsible to see that the fulness of the Christian faith is being communicated and understood.

This is even more critical in Ireland where the clergy are very much a force to be reckoned with. Most people still look to them as spokesmen for their community, as guardians of their way of life. In a land which so clearly needs a prophetic voice to recall the church to the fulness of the gospel it is natural first to look to those priests and ministers who are in daily contact with their people in the parishes. And it *is* a daily contact for, by English standards at any rate, the Irish clergy are very diligent visitors.

Wherever we look in the history of the church the clergy (as with the priesthood in the Old Testament) have sooner or later become guardians of the established order. It is all too easy for those of us who are ordained to speak the word of God to become so moulded by contemporary attitudes in both the world and the church that we do not even hear the word of the Lord clearly. As one American observer of the churches in Northern Ireland has remarked,

> Protestant and Catholic Clergy...have been conditioned by the same culture and history as their flocks. They also feel the weight of heavy community pressure. Any sign of reconciliation or offer of peace may be taken as weakness or straying from the faith and could bring on them the scorn of their own people.[2]

It follows that there is often a very real cost to face for any clergyman who would challenge the accepted patterns of his community and move out in love and reconciliation to include all, whatever their religious background. To adopt such a prophetic stance, to preach the wholeness of the gospel, is often done at considerable risk. I know of clergy, both Catholic and Protestant, whose homes have been attacked, or who have suffered all kinds of abuse from their own congregation because they have lived and preached the gospel of 'all one in Christ Jesus'.

With the cost so high it is clearly right that clergy should consider it carefully but, as always in the economy of God's kingdom, he who chooses anything less than God's way is always the loser. To preach half-the-gospel gets a very poor return, though in God's mercy it gets some. But for those who take the risk they find the guarantee of God absolutely firm.

> There is no man who has left house or wife or brothers or parents or children, for the sake of the Kingdom of God, who will not receive manifold more in his time, and in the age to come eternal life [Lk 18:29–30].

I remember how tentatively a Roman Catholic priest invited me to preach at an ecumenical service in his church in the week of prayer for Christian Unity. That is a rare event in Northern Ireland, and in his area it would be the first time anything like that had been tried. It was a risk, and he knew it. He had suffered attacks on his home by some from his own community because he was known to be 'soft on Protestants'. It was a decision he had taken entirely on his own. He had talked it through with his four curates. They were all sympathetic; they would all come; but none would share responsibility for the decision to hold the service. They were like Gamaliel—those who wait and see if God has said anything. The prophet is the one who says, 'God has spoken and this is what he requires us to do.' Gamaliel takes very few risks—the prophet risks all. So the priest was on his own.

He took all reasonable precautions and did not announce the service publicly. He telephoned the more open-minded Protestant clergy in his area during the few days before and then on the Sunday morning announced to each congregation at Mass that there would be an ecumenical service in church that afternoon. He was prepared to take the risk with his own congregation but as he said, 'I don't want to give an open invitation to our own bully-boys to come and make trouble.'

That Sunday afternoon I was in the vestry waiting for the service to begin. The parish priest was still apprehensive—he had been unable to sleep the night before and he was concerned that only a dozen or so would turn up.

Just after three o'clock we walked out into the church—it was packed to the doors with eight hundred people. As I preached on the cross of Christ breaking down barriers there was a general awareness of the power in what Christ had done for us. Afterwards over tea in the hall, conversations were not about the weather or the usual chit-chat, they were about the very heart of the gospel—the reconciling love of Christ. The risks had been real for the priest, but God had more than kept his promise of abundant blessing.

This costly service is, at heart, the way of the cross. For the Christian this always ends in the victory of the resurrection. There are times however when the joy and liberty of Easter seems a long way off. Many clergy have found that their ministry is like the seed falling into the ground and dying. Their sure confidence is that new life and consequent fruitfulness will follow. But, as with some seeds in nature, the time in the ground seems very prolonged.

Remembrance Day 1981 showed clearly how such a risk-taking prophetic ministry by a clergyman can pitch him into the heart of the agony of the cross. In the morning service he had preached on the necessity of forgiveness and reconciliation as a basic Christian response to conflict and division. It is a piercing and immediately challenging message to give and to hear when many in your area have been killed in the sectarian violence. But the congregation listened and quietly received this reminder of the very heart of the gospel message.

Later the same evening the minister heard an explosion. It was near-by and he was there in a few minutes. The man of the house was a part-time member of the security forces. His teenage son had gone out to put the car in the garage for the evening. It was booby-trapped. He was killed in the explosion—an innocent teenager, like many others, in the wrong place at the wrong time. There is no discrimination in a terrorist's bomb.

The minister was there as the pastor to bring the love and comfort of Christ. He was also there as that morning's preacher who had called for forgiveness and reconciliation. The father's question was obvious, 'What of your sermon now, Rector?'

The way of the cross is so demanding because the clergyman is part of the people who suffer. They also are hurt and they agonize over the brutality that strikes so often. Yet they are the ones who, fired by the resurrection hope, have to lead some of the most hurt and wounded into the Christian experience of love and forgiveness.

No story from the present troubles shows this as clearly as an episode in the ministry of the Rev. Sydney Callaghan. He is a Methodist minister who very courageously has led many others to discover fellowship in Christ across the divide. One afternoon in December 1973 he was called to see a Catholic friend, Jim Gibson, a local greengrocer. A few minutes before he arrived at the shop Jim had been shot by a Protestant who just shot and ran. Later that day he died in hospital. Love and anger fought with each other as Sydney wrote that same evening to the Belfast Telegraph. The letter was printed on the front page.

Dear young man, I am writing this letter to the paper in the hope that you may read it. Possibly you can't read, for there are some who would question whether somebody who would be capable of such a deed as you have committed would be intelligent enough to read.

If you can't read perhaps the friend who helped you, called in law an accomplice, might be able to read it to you for he is possibly more intelligent than you are, in that he is able to ride a motor bike and that takes a little more wit than pulling a trigger.

I am a Protestant clergyman. Along with others I have never failed to condemn violence of any sort from no matter what source it has come. That I unreservedly do again. Not, mind you, that that will mean much to you, for you are not impressed by anything we have to say.

But to keep the record straight it is spelt out again. I have also tried to serve people without regard to what their religious label may be. From the wastelands of the Shankill to the bleakness of Ballymurphy. From the deprived Falls Road to the affluent Antrim Road, people are people and the human heart is the same no matter in whose breast it beats.

I was in Jim Gibson's shop a few minutes after you left. I wish you could have shared what took place so that you might never forget. Because you were not there I will share with you some of the memories. There are others too intimate and personal to be shared with anybody outside the family circle. At any rate Jesus did say to be careful what you did with your pearls!

As I knelt on the floor beside him, some of the blood from the wounds you had caused spilt on my hands. There was no difference between his blood and mine although he was 'one of the other sort'. But then maybe you could have seen a difference for maybe you are the sort of person who says you can recognize the difference between 'our sort' and 'their sort'.

As I offered a prayer at the request of his pregnant wife I didn't hear a voice indicating that the God to whom I prayed was any different from the One we both worshipped in different ways Sunday after Sunday. That may surprise you—or maybe it wouldn't—as obviously you are not in touch with him at all as otherwise you wouldn't have broken his commandment which forbids us to kill.

As we waited in the hospital while the doctors fought for his life I didn't notice any difference in the tears we shed as we prayed for strength and consolation. Neither was it any easier or the grief any less when we gathered the family together with mother and broke to them the news that Daddy was dead.

As you are so strong and courageous why didn't you wait around to do this task yourself? Was it because you couldn't have borne what we had to bear or because, like a wild beast having attacked his prey, you had gone off into your lair? What sort of person are you?

You may pride yourself on your courage but it has no significance when placed alongside Mrs Gibson's. She carried herself with fortitude and by her strength gave her family resolution. She has no hatred in her heart towards you. She is sorry for you. Your actions reveal the depth of human depravity.

Her attitude reveals the measure of her Christian charity. She is bewildered but not bitter. You must be bitter and mixed up. We both tried to pray for you but it seemed to come easier to her which is a tribute to her spirit. It came harder to me for I was angry with a passionate anger. Perhaps I can now understand more fully how Jesus must have felt when he drove the money changers out of the temple.

Maybe it is wrong for me to feel angry with you for after all you are in part but a product of our sick society. Maybe the anger should be directed towards parents who teach their children to think in terms of 'them and us' and who nurture them in bigotry.

Maybe the anger should be directed towards education systems which divide and which emphasize a history which recognizes 1690 but not 1798, which eulogizes 1912 but despises 1916. Maybe the anger should be directed at churchmen who think in terms of narrow church structures but who are out of touch with one who taught to love our enemies.

Maybe the anger should be directed at politicians who bandy about words in public which incite to anger but who feather their own nests from the divisions which they help to perpetuate. Maybe the anger should be directed towards a society which is content to let things be with a disregard for the common humanity which binds us all together.

Maybe the anger should be directed towards myself, as a guilty reaction towards having done so little to make a community where all men shall be free to worship as their conscience dictates, are fulfilled in accord with their own abilities, and are encouraged to have their aspirations realized.

Whilst it is right that we should try to understand, nevertheless I must remind you that you are guilty and you bear personal responsibility for what you have done. I hope you are brought to justice. If not, and in the meantime, you will have to live with your own conscience. Through the long nights you will hear the sobs of broken-hearted people.

When you are being commended for your brave action you will hear another voice which condemns your wickedness. When your mind can no longer bear the torture of what you have done you will realize there is a justice written into the universe which cannot be tampered with and which has nothing to do with being caught and tried before men. Then perhaps you will realize that, 'God is not mocked: for whatsoever a man soweth, that shall he also reap.'

Your possible penitence then will be too late to bring back a man who was a good husband, a loving father, and a decent citizen whose only possible offence was that he was not identified with your group.

If there are others like you, then there are many of us who would say: if you cannot deal with your grievances in a mature and democratic way will you leave the rest of us to get on with learning to live together?

Otherwise we might die together and we would not want to be even found dead in your company.

It is hard to believe God loves you. But he does. It is hard to accept Christ died for you. But he did. Maybe if you would realize that and the implications of it for us all you might 'come to yourself' and discover his way for this province. Any other way leads to ultimate disaster.

Yours in Christian charity,
W. Sydney Callaghan

The 'way of Jesus' *is* the only way; 'any other leads to ultimate disaster'. It is the fearless proclamation of this message which ministers and priests are ordained to give. A prophetic ministry must take this message from the pulpit into the very heart of conflict.

Canon Harry Woodhead, an Anglican minister in Coleraine, has brought this full gospel to many in his part of the Province—to both Catholic and Protestant. We see in his ministry what happens when a clergyman is willing to step out—to take risks on the basis of the power of the gospel.

Joan Kane is just one who, through his ministry has been delivered from a life of bitterness and hatred. We pick up their story in July 1974, but first we must set the scene.

July 12th is the Protestants' day for celebrating. Their streets and homes are bedecked with Union Jacks, and the triumphal arches proclaim the victory of William of Orange over the Catholics in the Battle of the Boyne in 1690. The slogans proclaim 'No Pope'—'For God and Ulster'—'No Surrender'.

The bands are playing, the Orangemen parade, the drums beat out, and the banners that glorify King Billy's victory and Cromwell's massacre at Drogheda are proudly held aloft. The Orange rhymes say it all:

> Here's to the lily that dear Orange flower.
> Here's to the bright purple heather,
> The emblem of men who defied popish power,
> Here's to the Orange and purple together,
> So fill every glass; let the toast pass
> Down with popery, priest and the mass.

It's a great day for the majority in Ulster—it's a Bank Holiday, a time for a carnival. For many Catholics, it's like red rag to a bull.

On the eve of July 12th in 1974 Joan Kane, a housewife in her mid-thirties, had gone down to the bottom of her estate on the outskirts of Coleraine. Some Catholics had torn down one of the many Union Jacks, and had set fire to it. The Protestants gathered. The mood was ugly. The police were keeping both groups apart. Then along came the local rector, though Joan did not know who he was for she had stopped going to church many years before. He went and stood between the two opposing sides. He held out his arms to get their attention and stop the shouting. Then he prayed right there in the street and went on to invite people from both sides back in to his church to pray together.

Joan was dumbfounded. She was even more startled when she discovered that this minister was her new rector. 'God help us,' she thought, 'that's an apology we have for a minister! Fancy inviting Catholics and Protestants to come together and pray—we didn't want to know each other.'

Needless to say, she didn't join them for prayer. She went off home but although she would admit it to no one, she could not dismiss her new rector as easily as that. As she thought it over she began to realize some truths about herself, 'Joan, you think you're somebody who has great courage but there was a man who's going alone, with nobody to help him. He has more courage in his little finger than that whole crowd had between them.' And in spite of herself she began to admire him, though she could admit it to no one else for fear of letting the side down. From that day on she began to watch him.

She even started to go to church—just once a month—for she did not want to seem too keen! She expected very little from the church services. From her youth when she had been a chorister she remembered the utter boredom of the services. For her the prospect of going to church was like a prison sentence.

But, she now recalls, 'Every time I went it seemed that the minister was preaching to me and I didn't know that it was the Lord who was speaking.' And she began to feel guilty on account of the life she was living.

She remembered how she organized other women for the Protestant cause—how she rallied them behind the paramilitaries—how she encouraged the same hatred and bitterness for Catholics which was so deeply ingrained in her own heart.

There was one memory that came to her more often than most. Even today the thought of it brings tears to her eyes. It was the day she took her four year old daughter, Eleanor, on a march through Coleraine with the hooded men of the Protestant paramilitaries. 'We were showing off the armed men on whom we could count if the worst came to the worst.'

As the march moved off little Eleanor was holding on to her mother's skirt. 'Come on, straighten yourself up and march properly!' she told her daughter, for Joan was a proud and determined supporter of the UDA cause.

As the march neared its end Joan noticed that Eleanor

was no longer holding on to her skirt; she had gone. But she was not very far away, for there, a few yards ahead, four year old Eleanor was leading a section of the parade. With arms swinging and the hooded men behind her Eleanor showed all the commitment to the cause for which her mother worked so tirelessly.

It was a sight that stopped Joan in her tracks. It was a moment of truth and she made an immediate but heartfelt covenant with her Maker. 'God forgive me for what I have done to my own child. If I can get home without it hurting her in any way and with no bigotry put into that wee life, then I will never be involved in anything like this again.'

She never has been, and now, through her contact with Canon Woodhead she was beginning to see a better way. And then came the day when the power of God came to her in a way she had never known before.

As the rector was driving to a meeting in another town he felt that God was telling him to go and see Joan Kane. At first he dismissed the thought. 'It's just my imagination,' he felt. But, as the thought persisted and grew stronger, he became convinced that the Spirit of God was prompting him. He turned around and drove to Joan's house.

When he arrived Joan was on her knees making up the fire. She wouldn't get up as she was ashamed to show him the pain that continually wracked her body—she suffered badly with arthritis. As she stayed kneeling by the hearth she was dumbfounded as the rector said, 'Well, here I am, what have I come for?' Joan stared at him—it was obvious that he had gone crazy. But she said nothing. 'Are you sick?' he asked. Of course she was, but she did not want him to know about the arthritis so she merely confessed to a slight headache she was feeling.

By this time her arthritic pains were so bad that she had to get up, and of course her condition immediately became obvious. The rector asked, 'Would you mind if I laid on hands and prayed for healing?' She was very worried by this suggestion and totally confused. 'I know there is a God above,' she said, 'but I've locked him out. I believe God *could* heal me but I'm frightened it would only make me worse if you prayed for me. You see, I'm such a hypocrite. I've been involved in so many things that are wrong.' She didn't go on to tell the minister what she realized herself—that she wasn't a real Christian and, what is more, knew that she was not prepared to change enough to become one.

Harry Woodhead smiled: 'I feel that the Lord has sent me here for a reason this morning and I'd like to pray with you.' Joan was shaking as he read from the Bible and then prayed. As he laid hands on her head and prayed for the Lord to heal her she felt the warmth of God's healing power pass through her whole body.

The rector, already late for his meeting, bade a hasty farewell. She went with him to the front door and before he was through the gate she realized that every pain in her body had gone—in her hands, her head, her shoulders, her feet and her knees. She knew that God had healed her. She saw his power. She knew he was real. But, still, she wasn't going to surrender her life to him that easily.

During the next few weeks she went to church a little more regularly until one night in her own house she committed her life to Christ. She was now eager to discover all she could about the Christian life. She would often be round at the rectory asking question after question. She joined the weekly Bible study. She was committed to a new cause and she was as dedicated to the Christian way as she once had been to the old militant sectarianism.

Joan had been healed physically and she had committed her life to Christ. She was soon to learn that a much deeper healing had yet to take place in her life; a healing at the very heart of what reconciliation in Northern Ireland is all about. She no longer sang anti-Catholic songs, she no longer joined with the bully-boys. Her life wasn't dominated by anti-Catholic feelings, but one night she discovered just how deep the old bitterness had gone.

It was in the early days of charismatic renewal in Northern Ireland and the rector had arranged to hold a renewal prayer meeting in the parochial hall. Joan decided to go and see what it was all about. She sat down with the others—there were only a few in the semi-circle of chairs.

Just before the meeting was due to begin three nuns came into the hall. She can still remember the shock-waves that went through her body.

> You have no idea how I felt. I held on to that chair and I felt as though my knuckles would come out through the skin. All I wanted to do was to get up and hit them over the head with the chair. I was raging. I remember feeling that, after all, everything they said about the Rev. Woodhead was true—he's nothing but a Fenian-lover. Then the oldest nun stood up and read out of the Bible—I was disgusted! Here was a Catholic reading from a Bible—*our* Bible,—and her praying to *our* God. I used every curse word I could think of as I raged inwardly. When I ran out of these she was still reading and then she went on to explain the passage. I just had to listen. God forgive me, for she knew more about the Bible than I did who prized it as mine. She made it come alive to me. Then she prayed—I had never heard a prayer like it before. I couldn't pray like that. I said to myself, 'Joan, dear, there's something terribly wrong with you.'

When the meeting was over Joan went across to the nun and told her how she felt. She discovered that she was Mother Philomena, the Superior of the local convent. They embraced in the love of Christ. In the weeks that followed they became close friends and on many occasions Joan would go round to the convent to study the Bible—a former militant Protestant learning about the Bible from the Mother Superior of a Roman Catholic Convent. A miracle had happened and over those weeks God was exploring and healing many other deep areas of bitterness and sectarianism that had developed over the years.

As with the majority of Protestants, Joan had been brought up to believe that no Roman Catholic can be a Christian—that they are all bound for hell. It's a blindness that is seldom overcome by argument and persuasion. It is when a Protestant Christian is inescapably confronted with the love and power of Christ in a Roman Catholic, and there are thousands of them in Northern Ireland, that the old bigotry has to give way.

Joan was, by now, a very different person but she still knew there was more. She was struggling to live this new life in her own strength—and often she was making a mess of it. She began to understand that she must surrender her life to the Holy Spirit in a new way. The Mother Superior knew a depth of power and love in God's Spirit that she did not experience herself. She was a Christian but she longed to know, in reality, what it meant to be baptized in God's Spirit.

Her rector also knew that this was what she needed. He suggested that she come with him to a nearby weekend conference to hear the Rev. Cecil Kerr speak on the power and infilling of God's Spirit. She wanted to go but she had another engagement on the Saturday night when Cecil was speaking. 'What is this engagement that's so pressing?' the rector asked. Rather shame-faced she told how she had agreed to make the refreshments for the Vanguard meeting in nearby Limavady. Although she'd stopped marching with the extremists she still had a lingering desire to help 'her own side'. She was still supporting Mr Craig's Vanguard movement, which she considered more respectable than the UDA. She was being weaned gradually!

Harry Woodhead didn't protest but Joan thought that on Sunday morning after church he would try to persuade her to attend the last session of the conference in the afternoon. But he didn't. He passed no comment at all as she walked out of church.

'Well, if he couldn't even speak to me then I won't go!' She was defiant. Her pride was still causing her problems. She sat down in the afternoon to watch a film on the television. It was her husband (usually the one to wait quietly in the background) who burst through the shield that her pride had erected. 'You know why you're not going,' he told her quietly. 'It's the devil that's holding you back.'

She knew he was right and she asked him to drive her straight to the conference centre. As she entered Cecil Kerr was just beginning his address on the fulness of the Spirit. It was so plainly what Joan needed to know. As he was speaking she jumped to her feet. 'That's what I want,' she said aloud.

As they prayed with Joan she sensed the Holy Spirit filling her from head to toe and as she began to speak in tongues, she now knew that God had filled her with the power and love she would need so that she could continue in the work of reconciliation to which God had called her.

What has happened to Joan has happened to thousands of others. It is the heart of what God is doing in reconciliation in Northern Ireland. The bitterness and alienation is so deep that only a healing work of God's Spirit can solve the problem.

There are increasing numbers of priests and ministers like Harry Woodhead who see that it is this radical work of Christ that is needed—and have the confidence in God's Spirit to step out and take the risks of challenging the religious traditions which so easily trap people in both communities.

6. Faith, Hope and Love

Faith, hope and love must be brought out of the pages of the Bible, out from between the walls of churches, into the streets and into the hearts of all our people.

These are the words of Bishop Butler who throughout the seventies was the Anglican Bishop of Connor—the diocese that includes the northern half of Belfast and the whole of County Antrim. He said them in 1969. That was towards the beginning of the present troubles and also in the very early days of charismatic renewal in Ireland. The most noticeable feature of this spiritual renewal in both Catholic and Protestant churches has been the re-emergence in thousands of lives of a Christianity that is powerful, full of love, and bouncing with enthusiasm, that has blossomed amid an often weary tradition.

These past years of conflict have shown that the church is of no use to the world if the notions of faith, hope and love are simply beautiful chapters and uplifting doctrines between the leather covers of a Bible, nor if they are merely enshrined in stirring hymns, good sermons and moving liturgies within the four walls of a church building. Faith, hope and love are needed on the streets—and these troubled years have shown that they *only* get there if they are truly present in the hearts of people. This is what God has been doing in the renewing work of his Spirit, as Ireland has also experienced the beginnings of that significant outpouring of the Spirit which has been a feature of the life of the church throughout the world. It is as God renews his church that faith, hope, and love become deep realities in peoples' hearts and are then carried out into the streets.

In Ireland, as elsewhere, this move of God's Spirit has often been described as 'the charismatic movement'. This description *can* be helpful for it points to the central ideas of a gracious work of God and the empowering of God's people, in particular by the giving of spiritual gifts. On the other hand, it is misleading if it suggests that here is a movement or society within the church which Christians can join if they 'happen to like that sort of thing'.

What God is doing is *renewing his church*! Sometimes those who have been filled afresh with the Holy Spirit have given the impression that they now belong to a new club that has certain 'badges' to signify membership. This is doubly unfortunate for it encourages spiritual pride and elitism and at the same time devalues what God is doing. This outpouring of God's Spirit is not merely another 'good thing'—like the 'Samaritans' or the 'Legion of Mary'. It must also be said that there are people who feel uncomfortable with some of the things God is doing and consequently try to box these up into a 'movement' which can then safely be put to one side as 'not for me'.

It is undeniable that there have been many hurtful and clumsy things done and said by some who have begun to see how God is moving in his church in renewing power, and I would not want to defend these in others, or in myself. But what has become crystal clear to me since working for three years in Ireland is that the spiritual renewal of the church is an urgent need, it is something that God is doing, it is something that is radical, more radical than many who respond have yet realized, and it is something which the church ignores at its peril.

Already we have seen how God's Spirit has brought new depths of faith, hope and love to Al Ryan, John McKeown and Joan Kane. As God has worked to renew his church in Ireland over the last decade and more, he has done the same for many thousands of others—Roman Catholic, Anglican, Presbyterian, Methodist and the rest—priests, ministers, nuns and lay people. Throughout the country there are about five hundred meetings for praise and prayer —many of these are groups where both Catholics and Protestants meet together.

This ecumenical dimension is particularly evident in the conferences and rallies which have been a regular feature in Northern Ireland. Often several thousand come together for these events in Belfast and elsewhere. Perhaps one of the most significant of these in the early eighties has been the series of monthly praise services held in different churches in Belfast. These have attracted about a thousand on each evening, people from backgrounds as diverse as Roman Catholic, main-line Protestant denominations, and the newer house-churches or fellowships. These three traditions were represented on the leadership group that planned the services and their commitment was to recognize the importance of what God is doing in each. The overriding concern was that Christians should unite to become a people of praise and a people of power. The main thrust of the services has been so to praise God in the unity of the body of Christ, that the victory of Christ would be proclaimed over Belfast, a city that has seen ample evidence of the havoc caused when satanic forces are let loose.

Over the years it has become customary to hold a united service of praise in the open air on Pentecost Sunday. In 1982 this was held in a park in the heart of Belfast. It was a glorious sunny day and about three thousand people were there, Catholics and Protestants. It was an afternoon of praise and rejoicing that marked one of the church's major festivals. There was that extra note of joy because it was a united service—for such opportunities are rare in Northern Ireland. In fact, these 'renewal events' provide the only regular opportunities for significant numbers from both communities to come together, and then not just to meet and talk, which in itself would be a significant event in Northern Ireland. On these occasions they move out far beyond the culturally accepted norms—they pray together, they worship together, they hear God's word expounded and they express their love for one another.

The words of welcome from the platform caught the mood and expressed the commitment of the gathering, as could be told by the applause that punctuated the address.

We welcome you from many parts of Ireland for this rally to celebrate the Feast of the Pentecost. We come from many different traditions and backgrounds in this island. We come from North and South to proclaim that Jesus Christ is Lord! Amid all the noise and confusion of our world we proclaim that trust that can never change.

On the first Pentecost God's power was given to the early disciples of Christ. They were men and women just like you and me. They had the same problems of pride and prejudice that we have. Yet they believed the promise of God and allowed his Holy Spirit to invade their lives. As a result they went out to change the world. We are here today because they were faithful.

We want to say that what unites us is greater than that which divides us as followers of Christ in this island. We want to demonstrate Christ's love in truth and by our actions, in a spirit of mutual respect in order to call all men to recognize God as Father.

This is a day of celebration in the heart of Belfast. This is a day of joy because Jesus is alive. We believe that God gives us a *future* as we submit to his ways and obey his commandments. We believe that God gives us a *hope* as we trust in Christ's power to radically change our lives and our society.

Our hope is in Christ who alone can change our proud and stubborn hearts. We pray daily for a better way in this land. Political solutions are important but that alone will not solve the problem. The heart of the human problem is in the human heart. We can only have a new Ireland when we have new Irishmen—and only God can change our hearts. He is doing that all over the land and thousands are witnessing to it.

The congregation was obviously stirred by the welcome. It reminded them of the truth of what God had been doing over the past years. As they formed into small groups of four and five to pray together, they were witnessing to the most powerful answer there is for Northern Ireland's problem. Nuns and priests joined hands in prayer openly with ministers and Protestants from all over Belfast. It is something which the majority in Ulster would not do. There is still too much fear and suspicion. The conviction at the heart of the renewal movement is that a new Ireland is only possible with new Irishmen. The major task is one of conversion, new birth and renewal in the Spirit.

In the evangelical world of today it is fashionable to dismiss such statements as 'old fashioned pietism'. In recent years we have been made aware, and rightly so, of the social, economic and political dimensions in God's plan of salvation. It might, therefore, seem a step back into 'naïve evangelicalism' to proclaim that, before any adequate social or political solution can be found for Northern Ireland, a significant spiritual awakening is essential. But that is not so, for to assert the priority of spiritual renewal is to face the problem in the most radical way possible.

Some might say it is an easy option. Far easier, they argue, to say that a revival is what is needed than to spend endless and agonizing hours in thrashing out compromise and accommodations with opposing parties. Of course, to say, 'we want revival' and then to sit and wait for it is certainly easy, but that is merely using the phrase as a way of opting out of responsibility. It is no easy task if it is a true commitment. To accept that the fundamental need is for a spiritual awakening involves us in an extensive and demanding strategy. It demands a commitment to intercession and a costly involvement in the spiritual battle.

As is often heard, there is a hard core within Ulster's problem that is, in a very real sense, insoluble. The respective aims of either side are irreconcilable. The fears are based on a commitment to republicanism or unionism. It is a situation that does not allow compromise solutions or 'reasonable' schemes for accepting slightly less than each party would like. There is an all-or-nothing mentality at the root of the problem.

The radical answer is to see that the root must be changed; that fear and suspicion must be eradicated—to appease it is not enough. The commitment to the priority of a far reaching spiritual renewal in both communities has radical and far reaching implications. It acknowledges that only God can bring a solution to a problem whose twisted roots have been laid down in an inextricable tangle of satanic strategy which has been connived at by the English, the Irish Catholics and Ulster Protestants for over eight hundred years.

None of this excuses Christians from being deeply involved in working to alleviate society's many other ills. And Northern Ireland has more than its fair share—unemployment which in many places runs at 30%; alcoholism, a problem of massive proportions; the housing problem with its continuing ghetto-ization; and the problems of family life which is so much under pressure. There are many, though sadly not as many as there should be, who are becoming involved in such areas of need. But all of these are the results of the radical work of God, which by his Spirit brings about a new creation. And the fundamental make-up of a new creation is new creatures!

Stripped of all its human inadequacies and trivializations, spiritual renewal is evidence that God is working in this way in Ireland. There are, of course, many similarities between what God is doing through charismatic renewal in Ireland and what is happening in many other countries around the world. Several factors however stand out with particular relevance in Ulster, and they have to do with those three central experiences already mentioned—faith, hope and love.

1. A new reality of faith

Ireland is a land full of churches, and more than half-full of church-goers! By a big margin religion is a far more regular part of life than in any other western society. The churches are also far more traditional. A well-known international Christian speaker (who remains nameless in this context) says that whenever he gets off the plane in Ireland he becomes aware of the enormous weight of spiritual traditionalism descending like a blanket on him.

There are many reasons for this. Its very numerical strength means that the church can remain fairly 'successful' by concentrating most of its efforts on maintaining the tradition. Consequently, maintenance is a far more common attitude than mission, and this is so in all churches and denominations. Some years ago, for instance, I learnt how this is true within the evangelical tradition. I had preached to a congregation of about four hundred at a morning service in a noted evangelical church. Afterwards I asked the minister about the evangelistic involvement of the congregation. I imagined that the reason for the large number in church would be the personal evangelism of the church members. But, not so! I was told that the congregation's commitment to evangelism was virtually nil. They were 'sound', they 'believed the gospel', but because their church was full the minister found it very difficult to motivate them for evangelism.

The fact that the churches are a central part of the identity in each community, is a further reason for maintaining traditional attitudes. This means that the Roman Catholic Church in Ireland has changed far more slowly since the second Vatican Council than in most other parts of the world. There is even a strong awareness of differences of identity within the Protestant world. Presbyterians are jealous of their particular ways of doing things, and the Church of Ireland has made much of what it calls its peculiar 'Anglican identity'. Denominational particularity remains considerably stronger than is general in the rest of the western world in the late twentieth century.

As a result, many attend church out of custom, and for reasons of community identity, but the indicators are that the tide is turning. Many churchgoers find that traditional churchgoing has very few answers to give to the urgent questions raised by their society.

Through the renewal movement within the traditional churches many have discovered a new depth and reality in their faith. They have become aware of the bankruptcy of a Christianity that, having the form of religion denies the power of it (2 Tim 3:5). Molly O'Neill is just one among many thousands who have responded to this outpouring of God's Spirit. She is a Roman Catholic from Newry, a town that has seen much bitterness and many bombings and sectarian killings. Molly discovered the reality of God's love through personal tragedy.

After thirty years of marriage her husband, Owen, died suddenly. Her traditional faith could not cope.

> I turned against God. I now had no faith left. I felt, why did he take Owen away from me in the time of life when I needed him most? There obviously is no God.

Some friends took her to the prayer and praise meeting in nearby Rostrevor in the belief that Molly needed to meet with God in a new way. After a few short weeks she had discovered the healing power of God.

> When I was baptized in the Spirit my joy was completed. I had come to know God in a personal way. I realized that in taking Owen away from me he gave me something wonderful instead —his joy and his peace. And when I started to read the Bible, a thing I never did before, I began to realize that we're all one, that all of us (whatever our denomination) are God's children. It is only when all God's people come together that there will be peace in our land. Now I love to talk about the Lord, and share with others the joy and the praise that I have received. I thank God continually in singing for the day I really met him.

Her meeting with God had given Molly far more than comfort in her sorrow. It had changed her whole attitude to life, and particularly to the old religious traditions of Northern Ireland. As an immediate outcome of her new awareness of Jesus Christ, she began to display a real love for Protestants. She could now see them as fellow Christians, as members with her in the body of Christ. Her life is now part of the answer of Jesus' prayer, 'that they may be one... that the world may believe' (Jn 17:21). She never tires of giving witness to this essential unity between Christians, and through this, many have been caused to think again about their own attitudes, both to God and to one another.

Now, Monday by Monday Molly can be seen—usually on the front row—at the prayer meeting in Rostrevor, praising God with a joy and an enthusiasm which speak volumes. People come from all denominations and Molly is never more joyful than when she is praising God in the unity of Christ's body. Her favourite song is 'The Joy of the Lord is my Strength', and to see her singing this leaves no one in any doubt of its truth.

In Newry, where she lives, Molly is known by people on

both sides of the divide as someone committed to Christ and in whom they can see the love of God. Consequently, both Catholics and Protestants will come to her and ask for her to pray for them when they are ill or in trouble.

One of the marks in Molly's 'spiritual renewal' as with the majority of Roman Catholics (and not a few Protestants), is her discovery of the Bible as the living and active word of God. One of the deepest effects of spiritual renewal in Ireland is this hunger, evident in so many Roman Catholics, to learn from God's word. On one occasion I was in a group made up entirely of Roman Catholics. One lady told me that she had only recently started to read the Bible and that morning she had discovered, for the first time, that Jesus is coming back again. She had never consciously heard of this teaching before—though she must have heard reference to it many times in the liturgy of her church. But now, through the work of God's Spirit in her life, she was eager to discover the truth of God's word and she could not learn fast enough. Her question was straight to the point, 'Tell me *all* that the Bible says about Jesus' return to this earth. I want to know everything there is to know about it.' I thought of all the seemingly endless and normally fruitless debates I had known in my evangelical upbringing about *pre-*, *post-* and *a-* millennialism! Here in five minutes she wanted to know what the Bible taught. Teaching takes on a new directness in the presence of such hunger! It is also clear evidence of the promise of Jesus bearing fruit in our day. 'When the Spirit of truth comes, he will guide you into all the truth' (Jn 16:13).

In this discovery and renewal of personal faith God has plainly ignored our denominational distinctions. He has moved by his Spirit within both traditions and often has ministered his power and love through Protestants to Catholics and vice-versa. This not only shows God's disapproval of our divisions, it also reveals a little of God's sense of humour—as in this story, told by Cecil Kerr, of a businessman, one of the first Roman Catholics in Belfast to be involved in renewal.

> When a Protestant friend first spoke to him about the power of the Holy Spirit he became really interested and asked a Pentecostal pastor to pray with him that he might be baptized in the Spirit. The pastor who was so taken aback that a Roman Catholic should make such a request deferred the decision because he was really not sure that a Roman Catholic was fit material for the blessing! He took a week to think and pray and, thank God, he came back to pray with him and he received a real infilling of the power of the Holy Spirit. God has used him all over the North of Ireland to spread the good news of the power of Jesus Christ to save, to heal and to baptize with the Holy Spirit.[1]

These examples of renewed faith are multiplied by the thousand in Ireland today. It is a crucial part of God's sovereign work. For an increasing number of people faith is becoming an attitude of daily trust and expectancy. There is a growing wealth of evidence that supports the claim of Jesus—that the same works (and even greater) will be done in the age of the church than were seen in his own earthly ministry (Jn 14:12). Faith is being released from its static cerebral past when, for many, it merely described a commitment to a certain doctrinal position or, perhaps, referred to a particular moment of decision. Many are discovering the dynamic nature of faith and are being led to expect, and often to see, great things from God.

2. A discovery of *agape*-type love

'The greatest is love'.

A Christian couple had discussed what would be the wife's response if her husband were murdered—they knew this was a possibility as he was a member of the security forces. They were convinced that love is the only Christian answer to hatred and violence, though obviously they hoped and prayed that they would never have to face such a situation. In the event, they did, and it was a particularly harrowing experience for the wife. Her husband was killed but his body withheld by the terrorists for several days. In the interim she appealed publicly that there should be no retaliation, for as Christians, she said, we are called to respond to hatred with love.

At the funeral service, as husband and wife had previously agreed, the lesson was from Paul's first letter to the Corinthians. Rarely could those well-known words from Chapter 13 have echoed with such clarity in any church building: 'Love is patient and kind; love is not jealous or boastful; it is not arrogant or rude. Love does not insist on its own way; it is not irritable or resentful; it does not rejoice at wrong, but rejoices in the right. Love bears all things, believes all things, hopes all things, endures all things' (vv.4–7).

It is the *agape*-type love which we see in Jesus' death on the cross. It demands a response to hatred far beyond normal human capacity, so much so that we cannot demand it of anyone who has not discovered the reality of that kind of love in a personal encounter with Jesus.

Some years ago there was a sad interview on the television —one of many similar ones down the years—when the mother of a British soldier who had been murdered in Northern Ireland was asked, 'Could you ever forgive the men who did this to your son?' Her response was quiet, tearful but firm, 'No, never!' It is the understandable human response. It flows naturally from a mother's life-long care for her son. Everyone would do the same. The only force great enough to help us act otherwise is God's love that allowed Jesus to die on the cross for us who were so ungrateful that, at the time, we cheered in approval at his execution.

It is this kind of love, says St Paul, that is poured into our hearts through the Holy Spirit (Rom 5:5). It is perhaps the most moving testimony to the work of God's Spirit in Northern Ireland to see how many, with ample reason for hurt and bitterness, have discovered a freedom and ability to forgive as they have been healed by this love of God poured into their hearts.

For me, one of the most personally memorable demonstrations of this came on a bright sunny afternoon one December. With a couple of friends, I had driven over the border from Derry into Donegal. We stopped on a mountainside overlooking the beautiful view of Lough Swilly and together we had a time of prayer. The significance of this impromptu prayer meeting was that Sean was a Roman Catholic who had served a prison sentence, convicted of involvement with a republican paramilitary organisation. For my part, I was a clergyman, who, at my ordination within the Church of England, had sworn an oath of allegiance to 'Her Majesty, Queen Elizabeth, her heirs and successors according to law'. In many ways I stood for everything within the British establishment which Sean had been dedicated to bombing and shooting from the last inch of Irish soil.

But, when he was in the Crumlin Road prison Sean came to know Christ through reading the story of Nicky Cruz's conversion. He is still a Roman Catholic, and still a republican who wants the 'Brits out'. But now he acknowledges that violence is no way to achieve peace and justice. On that mountainside we both discovered that, however substantial our political, denominational or cultural divisions, the love of Jesus is powerful enough to penetrate all of these and make us brothers in God's family.

This love of God poured into our hearts by the Spirit heals even the deepest hurt. Often it is like ointment applied to a wound that penetrates more and more deeply until a full healing takes place. Many in Ireland have discovered the need for this love of God to be applied afresh as they discover that the wound has gone deeper than they had previously realized.

A few months after my arrival in Ireland I was speaking at a day of Renewal in a Roman Catholic church. During the tea break a young nurse, with tears in her eyes, came up to speak with me. She told me how she had been brought up a Catholic in Belfast to hate Protestants but that when she had come to know the Lord a few years previously, all this hatred had been taken away by the operation of God's love in her life. The reason for her distress on this occasion was that she had discovered new areas of bitterness which had been so deep that they had not yet been healed. 'When you were speaking,' she told me, 'I could not listen to you. As I heard your English accent I felt a fierce anger welling up inside me. I had been healed from my hatred of Protestants but I realize now that I still have a deep resentment against the British, and I want God to heal me of that, too. Would you pray with me?' As we prayed, God, by his Spirit, poured his love afresh into her heart and she knew a release from that root of bitterness which had penetrated so deeply.

It was this work of God's Spirit that made it possible for us to go back into the church, to join hands together and sing, with deep conviction:

Jesus stand among us at the meeting of our lives,
    Be the sweet communion at the meeting of our eyes,
Jesus we love you and as we gather here,
    Join our hearts in unity and take away our fear.

So to you we're gathering out of each and every land,
    Christ the love between us at the joining of our hands,
Jesus we love you and as we gather here,
    Join our hearts in unity and take away our fear.[2]

3. A future and a hope

Hope is in very short supply in Northern Ireland. The political situation is so log-jammed, and the cultural and religious prejudices so deep that hope is a very rare commodity. There is a church in the southern part of the Province that has a stained glass window whose three sections depict faith, hope and love. Some years ago a bomb exploded in the telephone exchange nearby and shattered the middle one of these three windows. Hope had gone. It is a parable of what has become true for many people and situations in Northern Ireland.

There are many Christians (and non-Christians) who are working valiantly in many different ways to reconstruct hopeful signs for the future. The Corrymeela community is perhaps the most well-known example. What has come through loud and clear in the Spirit's work of renewal in Ireland is that God approves such efforts, and, most importantly, he himself is working to bring about a future and a hope—for he is the God of all hope.

In the Scriptures one of the vehicles for hope is the word of God through prophecy. The restoration and growth of this ministry in the renewing work of God's Spirit has become one of the major sources of hope among Christians in Ireland.

Many of the prophecies given in united gatherings over the years have spoken of that hope that God is injecting into the situation. At the National Charismatic Conference in Dublin in 1976 came these words:

> Bring to me your broken bodies that I may uplift and heal. Bring your drooping spirits. Bring to me your broken hearts. I can change those hearts of stone and give you hearts of flesh. Come and be empowered by the Holy Spirit. Come and listen to what he is saying. Come and pray the prayer that he inspires. The Holy Spirit will be with you to counsel and care. You are

an orchestra. You are an army. I am uniting you in my Spirit. When you are fully united I will use you to answer your prayers. Walk with me—my love for you knows no bounds.

It bears many of the marks of how God spoke to the people of Israel during their period of Exile in Babylon:

Comfort, comfort my people, says your God. Speak tenderly to Jerusalem and cry to her that her warfare is ended, that her iniquity is pardoned, that she has received from the Lord's hand double for all her sins (Is 40:1–2).

It is a message that Ireland needs to hear, and continue to hear, for it is very difficult to hold on to hope when, humanly speaking, so many of the indicators continue to show a deepening hopelessness. The Christian in Ireland who is looking to hear what God is saying must continually wrestle with this problem. The psalmist knew well the conflict between hope and despair:

I say to God, my rock: 'Why hast thou forgotten me? Why go I mourning because of the oppression of the enemy? As with a deadly wound in my body, my adversaries taunt me, while they say to me continually, "Where is your God?"' Why are you cast down, O my soul, and why are you disquieted within me? Hope in God; for I shall again praise him, my help and my God (Ps 42:9–11).

While many have continued to rejoice in the new signs of hope that God is bringing through the outpouring of his Spirit, others have naturally tended to doubt—some who have themselves tasted the renewing work of the Spirit, and others who are watching from the sidelines, perhaps curious, or sceptical or even hostile. As I have reflected over these past few years on this 'hope given, and hope seemingly delayed' I have noticed how this is consistent with what we know of

God's dealings with his people in the Scriptures. We discover that the hope and the future which God promises involves quite a process of rediscovery, healing and rebuilding which, in itself, becomes bewildering if we do not continually fix our eyes on the heart of God's promise.

So it was for the people of Israel in their return from Exile. The heady days of excitement on hearing that their 'warfare is ended' seemed to fade somewhat in the hard reality of the return. It was no triumphalist re-entry, once for all, into the promised land. There were different waves of returning exiles over a number of years followed by fits and starts in the rebuilding of the city, the walls, the temple and their new religious life. As I have pondered the patterns of God's work of renewal and restoration in Ireland, the books of Ezra and Nehemiah have suggested many clues that help in discerning what God is doing.

These two books depict the struggle that is often involved in entering into the promised hope. Following the initial edict of Cyrus, when he sent many Israelites back to the promised land to rebuild the temple, the days of 'heady enthusiasm' began. 'Then rose up the heads of the fathers' houses of Judah and Benjamin, and the priests and the Levites, every one whose spirit God had stirred to go up to rebuild the house of the Lord which is in Jerusalem' (Ezra 1:5). It was not the whole nation who left—they would enter later into the fulness of God's plan—but those whom God prompted. The exhilaration of this initial wave of exiles when they reached Jerusalem was understandable. Straightaway they built the altar of the Lord and spent seemingly endless time in the praise and worship of God (Ezra 3:1–6). They had not been able to do this for seventy years—in deep anguish of heart they had hung up their musical instruments during the pain of exile.

As a nation they had been through the experience of 'the dark night of the Soul'. At first, on their return, they were not immediately involved in any major rebuilding and reconstruction. That would wait; to begin with, they simply wanted to praise God.

But rebuilding could not be put off for ever. 'From the first day of the seventh month they began to offer burnt offerings to the Lord. *But the foundation of the temple of the Lord was not yet laid*' (Ezra 3:6). Rebuilding now became the order of the day, and it was this that was to prove the testing time—holding on to the clear promise from God about hope and the future in the midst of enormous obstacles. They learned about the battle involved in rebuilding. They discovered that there were many who wanted things left exactly as they were (Neh 6). They found it necessary to be both builders and warriors at the same time. They learned God does no new work, nor does he move from one stage to the next in his plans for us, unless the foundation is solid. That foundation must be true repentance in the people of God (Ezra 9; Neh 9). They learned the demands of spiritual discipline, in particular the importance of prayer and fasting (Ezra 8:21–23; Ezra 9:3–5; Neh 1:4). They had to learn, by their mistakes about how to live in love and justice with one another (Neh 5).

The prophet Haggai brought the Lord's word to the people as they were learning these lessons. He faced them squarely with the lack of blessing which had become a feature of their life.

> You have looked for much, and, lo, it came to little; and when you brought it home, I blew it away. Why? says the Lord of Hosts. Because of my house that lies in ruins, while you busy yourselves each with his own house. Therefore the heavens above you have withheld the dew, and the earth has withheld its produce (Hag 1:9–10).

The people were guilty of wrong priorities. They had

stepped out into God's future but somewhere on the way they had held back from one of the most crucial tasks involved in their return to the fulness of his blessing—the rebuilding of the house of the Lord. But the Lord assured them that if they returned to the central priority he would restore the fulness of his promise.

> Take courage, all you people of the land, says the Lord; work, for I am with you, says the Lord of Hosts, according to the promise that I made you when you came out of Egypt. My Spirit abides among you; fear not. For thus says the Lord of Hosts: once again, in a little while, I will shake the heavens and the earth and the sea and the dry land. ... The latter splendour of this house shall be greater than the former, says the Lord of Hosts; and in this place I will give prosperity, says the Lord of Hosts (Hag 2:4–9).

In the early days of renewal in Ireland the Lord gave a picture to a group of national leaders of an incomplete spider's web over Ireland through which they discovered that God was revealing the manner of his working—that he was at work silently throughout the whole land, and that it was the leaders' task to watch carefully and recognize the pattern of his plan as it unfolded. It would seem that this stage is coming to completion and that now the call is to move forward into rebuilding and restoration.

In 1981, at a National Conference for leaders in spiritual renewal, the word from God recalled them to this central message of hope with a promise of yet greater blessing than had been seen so far.

> The word that I speak to you this weekend is a word that makes you ready for my purposes. I am speaking to you because I have called you and have plans for you. Behold I am going to send a revival in the power of my Spirit, and I am preparing the leadership that will lead that revival, and there are many others

whom I will call and prepare, that the power of my Spirit may not be wasted, but may be channelled and may be productive in many lives and in many communities.

The message is that the renewing work of God's Spirit that has been going on in Ireland since the early seventies has been but a preparation for the greater thing that God wants to do. There had been an awareness for some time that the initial 'headiness' and verve of charismatic renewal had not moved forward as many thought it might. The call of this leaders' conference, at the beginning of the eighties, was to a realization of the reality of the spiritual battle, and the disciplined commitment needed in order to see the victory of Christ. There was a significant emphasis on the need for fasting and intercession for the nation.

It was a conference that placed a definite responsibility on the leaders. It is their task to enable others to hear what God is saying. Some of them, who have been diverted from the central priorities, need recalling to the thrust of God's plan, others need to realize the continual commitment and discipline that is needed in the spiritual battle. All are being called from the heady days of rejoicing when they have not been concerned with rebuilding. Perhaps some have felt God's promise was fading because they have sought to prolong forever the 'Let's just praise the Lord' phase.

What had happened along the way—had it simply been a question of God not doing everything all at once? Had it been a lack of spiritual discipline? A lack of effective leadership?—or wrong priorities? No doubt it has been a mixture of all of these but the picture from the prophet Haggai reminds us of the ever present danger in what we do with God's blessings. God's main complaint was that the Israelites were using *his* blessings to further *their* ends—'Is it time for you yourselves to dwell in your panelled houses, while this house lies in ruins?' (Hag 1:4).

The people knew that the Lord's desire in bringing them back from exile was that the temple should be rebuilt. In the event they had derived enormous benefit from the return—they had well-built houses to live in—but they put off the rebuilding of the temple; they kept saying, 'the time has not yet come to rebuild the house of the Lord' (Hag 1:2).

In Ireland there has been a tendency to receive the blessings of the renewing work of the Spirit and then be diverted into enjoying it within the 'old house'—the well-known denominational structures. The whole set-up in Ireland makes it so difficult to cross the barriers. To begin with there are the sheer physical problems of 'ghetto-type' housing situations. It is also undeniable that one's own 'denominational buddies' find renewal more difficult if it includes the idea of reconciliation. Consequently, it is an attractive option to develop 'our renewal' first, to say that it is not time yet to build the house of the Lord—the body of Christ without our disfiguring denominational wounds.

God's message is that it is not possible to continue to enjoy the fruits of his renewing work without keeping to his priorities and remaining in step with his timetable. God's concern is with rebuilding his house—and significantly, the title of the Belfast renewal conference over Whitsun weekend in 1981 was 'Building the Body of Christ'. The purpose of God in renewing his church is restoration and perhaps in Ireland, more clearly than anywhere else, this involves an abandonment of our old divisions, and a commitment to reconciliation within the body of Christ.

If the people are faithful to the original vision, Haggai assures them that the future will be far more glorious than the past has ever been. This same pattern can be seen in a picture shared at the 1981 leaders' conference. It was of water lilies growing in a lake with a river flowing nearby. As the river begins to rise through flooding, the lake is swallowed up into the flood waters which then flow on, bringing new life into dry areas far away, so that the whole land is fed and watered. The person sharing this picture explained its meaning:

> I believe that the Lord is saying to us that he wants us even to lay down the beautiful things that he has given us, the blessings that he has brought us, and not to keep them secluded in the places where we can enjoy them but to allow the river of his Spirit to take us together into the greater purpose that he has for us to share, in the fuller thing that he wants to do for his glory and for extending his kingdom.

All prophecy must, of course, be tested, but the history of the outpouring of God's Spirit so far has confirmed the truth of much of what has been said. Many thousands have found release, healing, and reconciliation through what God has been doing. But the greatest task yet remains—the transformation of society through the people of God thus filled by the Spirit. That is the hope which God inspires.

7. A Sign of Hope

The renewal of the church in Ireland is faced with a particular problem. Many who would be happy with personal spiritual renewal, even denominational spiritual renewal, turn away when they see that this involves fellowship across the religious divide.

This creates a dilemma. Spiritual renewal will always lack its central thrust and convicting power if it is divorced from reconciliation within the broken body of Christ. As long as people's only knowledge of what God is doing is confined to a particular manifestation in a one-church-denominational setting they will experience only a fraction of the power and significance of renewal. Yet the whole structure of Ulster's society, as well as the heavily defended nature of each denominational fortress, makes it very unlikely that many would ever witness a full expression of what God is doing. It became essential that there should be some way to demonstrate the twin movements of renewal and reconciliation in one place, as a sign of hope.

In 1974 a group of Christians in Belfast believed that God was calling them to respond to this need. They sensed that God was leading them to establish a Christian community of both Catholics and Protestants that would provide a clear example of what God intended for his people. It would provide a centre to which people could come from all over

Ireland and experience a common life of prayer and sharing together, whatever their denominational background.

Eventually a large Victorian mansion was purchased on the shores of Carlingford Lough—on the border between North and South, and the Christian Renewal Centre was founded. From the beginning it has been a venture of faith and the whole financing of the community and its work has been based on a promise given by God at the very beginning —that he would put it into the hearts of the right people to give the right amount of money at the right time. From the very first day of its existence, the community has always found that God has been faithful to that promise. They have never appealed for money but have consistently known the provision of God as more than adequate for all their needs.

Rostrevor is situated in one of the most beautiful parts of Ireland, where the Mountains of Mourne come down to the sea. The naval vessel anchored off-shore is a permanent reminder that the surrounding border area has known some of the worst violence over the past years.

As in so many new ventures of faith God has used one man to spearhead this work—the Rev. Cecil Kerr. He is recognized by many throughout Ireland as someone who has been used by God in the ministry of reconciliation. To a large extent, his conviction that reconciliation is central to God's work of renewal, arises out of his own experience.

I was brought up in a rural part of Northern Ireland in a community which is almost equally Roman Catholic and Protestant. Like most Protestants in Northern Ireland my forbears had come over from Scotland and England in the early seventeenth century during the Plantation under James I. When they came they took over the good land from the native Irish who were largely Catholics.... That was three hundred years ago but it might have been yesterday. That invisible wall of mistrust has remained over the centuries only becoming visible

when circumstances combine to bring hostility into open conflict...deep down there is that invisible barrier of mistrust
lodged deep within our hearts like a steel shutter which extends
to an area of the brain and cuts off from rational argument and
discussion. Deep down it is this which stands in the way of
'power-sharing' and co-operation at a level where I am
threatened on the point of my existence....This is the root of
the problem and it is a root firmly grounded in the hard earth of
Irish soil. All attempts to reach political solutions must take
cognizance of this fact. And it is precisely here where politics or
man-made solutions will always fail....The more fundamental
problem needs more basic remedies. The heart must be changed
and I know only one power that can change the human heart—
the power of God through the reconciling love of Jesus Christ.
...This is what God is able to do by his Spirit in our land today.
As I speak with our politicians and hear them talk I realize the
awful dilemma they are in. It's like a log jam and they cannot
find a way out, and there is no way out till we can forgive one
another and accept one another. And we cannot forgive one
another till we allow God to forgive us. This is at once the
simplest and yet the most difficult thing we shall be called on to
do. But if we do not do it we perish. We must find a way to live
together or we shall die together....I firmly believe, because I
know it in my own experience and in the experience of many
others that God can come in the power of his Holy Spirit and so
work in my heart that he can melt away the hatred of the
centuries and give me ground for hope and trust. He can
liberate me from the prison houses of the past into a far more
glorious future.[1]

God has used Cecil Kerr to lead a work in Rostrevor
which has enabled thousands over these years to discover
that same reconciling love of God. The widespread suspicions that many had when it was first founded are
beginning to disappear. There remain some, particularly
those from the more 'right wing' Protestant groups, who
would describe the work as a satanic deception. But the

general attitude is more like that of Gamaliel—'If it's of God it will prosper, but let's wait and see.' I met one of these contemporary Gamaliels when I was conducting a service in a church not far from Rostrevor. After the service he spoke very warmly to me and expressed his admiration for the work of the Renewal Centre. When the work at Rostrevor first began he had made his own position clear. 'It might be of God, but that is difficult to believe as there are Roman Catholics involved. Only time and evident spiritual results could convince me that this is a true work of God. I'll give it ten years.' Such is this pace of change in the Irish church! But as he spoke with me he confessed that over the years since the founding of the Renewal Centre he had seen much evidence of the power of God through its ministry. Already, two years ahead of his own time schedule, he had reached the conclusion that it was a very significant work of God.

The community itself is made up of Christians who commit themselves for a year or more to the central vision of the work which is threefold—to be a place of prayer, a place of renewal and a place of reconciliation. These aims mould the kind of community it has become. It is clearly not 'a community for community's sake'. It is not there primarily for the growth or healing of the individual members, though this has been an important factor for many. Primarily, it is an 'apostolic' community. A group with a mission, though central to that mission is the demonstration by its own lifestyle of what an ecumenical Christian community means in practice.

1. A place of prayer

First and foremost it is a community of prayer. The focus of this prayer is an hour morning and evening when the community, and any guests, join for a time of praise and worship, meditation on God's word and intercession. Every community down the years develops its own spirituality, and the Rostrevor community is no exception. Its tradition is based on the conviction that effectiveness in intercession comes as Christians commit themselves to a life of praise and worship. There is a central nerve to their praying which says, 'Nevertheless, we *will* praise God.' It is the same determination which we see in the prophet Habakkuk: 'Though the fig tree do not blossom, nor fruit be on the vines, the produce of the olive fail and the fields yield no food, the flock be cut off from the fold and there be no herd in the stalls, *yet I will rejoice in the Lord,* I will joy in the God of my salvation' (Hab 3:17–18).

As they meet twice daily the news has so often been of more bombings and killings; of renewed rioting, or of yet another sign of political hope thrown on the scrap heap of bigotry. It would be very easy for prayer to spiral down into the whirlpool of human hopelessness and powerlessness. But at the heart of their communal prayer is the Godward note of praise and worship. There is a deliberate refusal to give in to the blackness and despair around. God's name is to be uplifted and exalted; the lordship of Christ must be acknowledged. They enter into praise and worship as the way of proclaiming the victory of Christ. It is as the praying community stand in that place of victory that intercession becomes an effective weapon in the spiritual battle.

It is into this atmosphere of prayer that any guests come to share. Many come for healing—physical and emotional. Although it is not specifically a home of healing, the healing ministry has become one of the notable marks of its work. Their conviction is that wherever a believing community commits itself to praise and prayer the victory of Christ over sickness and disease will be evidenced time and time again. Often, as someone has come for prayer-ministry it has not only led to a healing of their illness—it has meant that, for the first time, they have prayed openly together with Christians from the 'other side of the divide'. Perhaps the person who laid hands on them was someone of whose salvation they would previously have been very doubtful, simply because of their denominational background. A sign that every part of God's work involves recognition of the oneness of Christ's body.

2. A place of renewal

The community is committed to renewal within the traditional churches. 'We have no desire to start another denomination,' they say, 'it's the last thing that Ireland needs.' It means that much of their work involves leading missions and retreats in local churches in the belief that God has a purpose for these; he does not want to bypass them, though the reminder is often given that if the traditional churches resist what the Spirit is doing then God, in his sovereignty, could well move into other channels.

Central to this work of renewal in the churches is their ministry to clergy, seen most clearly in their conferences and days of renewal for clergy. These provide an opportunity for clergy to step aside from the demands of their own community to meet afresh with God for themselves. Many will come from areas where the 'troubles' are an ever present dimension in their pastoral ministry. But the emphasis is not so much on handing out a spiritual treat on a plate. Rather the days offer a setting in which clergy can minister to one another. The community feel this is one of the most vital services they can offer to clergy in a society which exalts its priests and ministers and puts them on a pedestal. Many demands are made upon them; but rarely would a congregation consider their pastor's spiritual needs. At Rostrevor the visiting clergy are encouraged to share honestly and openly with others there; to ask for prayer and ministry for themselves; and to join in a shared prayer-ministry to each other.

Often, as a result of such contacts with clergy, small teams from the community are invited to lead a renewal week in a local church—to 'take on' the massive weight of traditionalism! As yet, there are only a few churches that have moved forward, as entire congregations, courageously to follow the Spirit's lead in renewal. It is a patient pain-staking work that is needed. And always one eye is kept open to the dimension of reconciliation which can never be omitted entirely even if, at the time, the main emphasis is on one local denominational congregation.

One of the issues that constantly emerges is the need for a radical rethink about ministry. In both Protestant and Catholic churches the Irish clergy still 'do it all' in a way that is much less common in many other countries. The need to develop shared leadership in local churches and then the development of the gifts to every member in the congregation is one of the greatest challenges that faces every local church.

For churches as traditional as those in Ireland, renewal is often seen as a massive threat. It will need much courage on the part of leaders, both ordained and lay. It will need the kind of courage of which Cecil Kerr wrote:

> I have often longed at church gatherings, synods and councils, when we are debating questions relating to our faith as if we were in a debating chamber, to stand up and ask the whole audience to stop and spend an hour together in prayer before we proceed. I have often wondered what would happen if one had the courage to do that![2]

3. A place of reconciliation

Psalm 133 is often heard at conferences, prayer meetings, retreats and weekends of intercession which are a regular part of the work at Rostrevor: 'Behold, how good and pleasant it is when brothers dwell in unity...there the Lord has commanded a blessing, life for evermore.' Many down the years have testified to a deeper awareness of God's power and love when they have come into an atmosphere of praise and prayer in which Catholics and Protestants join as one.

If prayer could be described as the *basis* of the work, and renewal as the *means,* then reconciliation is the *aim* that inspires the whole community. They see their work as part of the eternal purpose which God set forth in Christ, 'as a plan for the fulness of time, to unite all things in him, things in heaven and things on earth' (Eph 1:10). From Paul's same letter to the Ephesians comes his teaching on reconciliation which has become the community's 'theme text'.

> For he is our peace, who made us both one, and has broken down the dividing wall of hostility...that he might create in himself one new man in place of the two so making peace, and might reconcile us both to God in one body through the cross, thereby bringing the hostility to an end' (Eph 2:14–16).

Just as in Paul's day when 'the Jews had no dealings with the Samaritans', so the power of the cross is the heart of the work of reconciliation. It is this message of Calvary that is at the centre of the community's work—even though the Renewal Centre is known for its testimony to the power of the Spirit, there is never any wavering about the source of all power, and victory and love—that is found in the cross of Christ as nowhere else.

If this were an account of the history of the community (which it is not) I would need to make more than a passing reference to the day by day 'reconciliations' that are part of any community's life. There are plenty of these—and at very ordinary and human levels! Every member of the community brings not only a personality and gifts which enrich the others and strengthen the work—everyone also brings weaknesses, hurts and irritating little foibles which can make life very hard for others. But one thing is a feature for all community members. They are learning to live with Christians of another tradition and to come to terms with a form of Christian expression which is often markedly different from the one they have always known and experienced.

During my three years as a member of the community I was often asked by visiting Protestants, 'What do you *really* feel about the Roman Catholic Church?' Some asked this question in sheer amazement at what they had seen at Rostrevor. They could not take it all in—Catholics and Protestants worshipping, praying and studying the Scriptures together with such an evident lack of 'aggro' that it was impossible to tell which was which (and to many Ulster people that can be irritating in itself!). What they saw so often challenged to the roots their whole view of Christianity as well as their cultural patterns.

Usually I encouraged people to allow the evidence to speak for itself. There were Roman Catholics whose salvation was so evidently real that to doubt it was like wondering whether Billy Graham was an atheist! I encouraged them to go away and pray through what they had seen—perhaps God had shown them some things which were going to demand a considerable amount of demolition work in the area of inherited denominational systems.

'But what about the Council of Trent?' they would sometimes ask, 'We all know the Church of Rome hasn't changed fundamentally.' Here I point to the second Vatican Council and tell them some of the things that the Roman Catholic Church said then—and since—which testify to the radical strand of biblical thinking which informs so much of that Church's teaching and action now. I confess that, if I do a witch hunt, I can still find statements in the past and the present which contradict some of the things *I* am most pleased about in their other statements. But my basic conviction is that the changes within the Roman Church are evidence to me of the work of God's Spirit of Truth. It will take a long time until they *and we* change enough to bridge the chasm created over four hundred years. That it has begun to happen as quickly and radically as it has, is to me a sign of God at work.

Sometimes I have had to ask a fellow Protestant, 'Are you sure you want God to change and work in power within the Roman Church? Is it making things a little too uncomfortable for you? Is it too much to contemplate the threat this poses to your own tidy little world view?' It can sound a bit harsh put down in this way, but an unwillingness to see God doing what, deep down, we would rather not see him doing, is sin, and it must be challenged.

'Okay. But surely they're wrong in their attitude to priests. Jesus himself said we should call no man "Father".' It is my conviction that *both* of us have made big mistakes about ministry. As a Protestant I obviously believe the Reformation doctrine of priesthood and ministry is more biblical. But I don't believe the Reformation was thorough enough at this point. Most Protestant churches in practice have a very separated heirarchical ministry where the minister is 'Jack of all trades'. In fact, in the majority of Roman Catholic churches in Ireland there is far more lay participation in leading the service than you find for instance in most Presbyterian churches. Protestants may not call their ministers 'father' but often he is treated like a 'tin-god'.

I often recount the story of the time I was meeting for Bible study with a group of Roman Catholics. One lady who was fairly new to the group asked me, 'Father, I read yesterday that Jesus said that we should call no man father. That confused me—does it mean that it's sinful to call a priest "Father"? What do you think, Father?' From her use of the word, she would obviously find it very difficult to stop the habit of years! But what an opportunity for a Protestant minister to be given. However, I had no desire to make a sectarian point. I explained to her that none of us, whatever our tradition, believed that this text of Jesus should be taken in a bald literal way. After all, everyone calls someone 'Father'—primarily our own human father. Jesus himself seemed quite happy with this. He was teaching that the place of God is unique and that our human ways of speaking should always preserve that uniqueness. We should never so exalt a person by what we call him that we demote God in the process. We should never use the words 'Lord', 'Father' or 'Reverend' if that exalts a human being into a position that belongs to God alone. The important issue therefore is the way in which we use the word 'Father' and what we imply both about the clergyman and about God. I concluded by suggesting that if she continued to call her clergyman 'Father' she should never do it in such a way that isolated him from fellowship with others—at times she should call him 'brother' or Sean—because, before he is a clergyman, he is a member together with her in God's family.

'Well then, what about praying to the saints and the Virgin Mary?'—that normally comes. And I frequently reply by sharing with them my conversation with a Catholic member of our community. There are Roman Catholics I know who no longer make any petitions to the saints, but Terry still found it a valuable part of his own prayer life. He explained it like this. 'As Catholics we don't pray to the saints like we pray to God. It's God who gives answers to prayer, not the saints. But just as I might ask you to pray for me when I'm ill, why can't I ask one of the saints in heaven to pray for me as well?' Put in that way, it is far more understandable for Protestants, and the *hackles* should not rise, even though there are still differences. At the time, I said to Terry, 'Well, I have no particular difficulty with that. I see that it takes very seriously the communion of the saints, and that it doesn't detract at all from prerogatives that should be given to God alone. I don't see anything wrong with asking saints in heaven to pray for me—it's a nice thought to think that one of them might, but my problem is that I'm not sure the saints can hear me if I ask them!'

It is when we are able to talk through issues with our fellow Christians in this relaxed way that our appreciation both of their faith and ours is deepened and extended. It is this openness and listening that creates trust and thus defuses our defensive attitudes, our suspicions and our fears. Protestants, particularly in Northern Ireland, need to listen again to what the Pope said at Drogheda and ask, 'Am I sure? Can't I begin to trust him as a brother in Christ?'

> May no Irish Protestant think that the Pope is an enemy, a danger or a threat. My desire is that instead Protestants would see in me a friend and a brother in Christ.

There will remain doctrinal differences between Christians. This has been part of the sadness of the church's history from the second day of its existence until now. There are still great issues of principle on which we need to stand but there are many Roman Catholics today who could lead many Protestants to discover what it means to be saved by the grace of God as we put our trust in Christ. There are many who have a deep love of God's word and a commitment to evangelism to a degree that makes many Protestants seem lukewarm. And above all the Spirit is making into one what we have torn apart.

Herein lies Ireland's hope. It is its involvement in this ministry that makes the Renewal Centre a sign of that hope. Cecil Kerr expresses the community's central conviction.

We are convinced that it is only as we come together at the foot of Christ's cross and receive his reconciliation which we can never deserve or earn that we are inseparably made one in him. Unity at the cross transcends every barrier of religion, race and class. It is this miracle of reconciliation which God is effecting by his Spirit. Not all our questions are answered nor all our problems immediately solved, but we find there is a love released at the cross which destroys every barrier that Satan can erect. For years we have impoverished each other by our separation, and now we are beginning to learn what wonderful riches our heavenly Father has given us to share with each other. In a thousand simple, yet profound ways God works in the hearts of those who meet here to break down the walls that centuries of fear have built. We know that this work is a direct attack on the kingdom of darkness, for it is Satan's intention to sow mistrust and fear and to create havoc and destruction. The past years have taught us how much we are involved in the front line of this spiritual warfare, but we praise God that Jesus Christ is Lord over all the powers of evil.

8.   Who Will Make the First Move?

> We have to confess that our churches have become fortresses
> that separate us from one another instead of the house of God
> where we can kneel in mutual forgiveness.
>
> (Cecil Kerr)

To any impartial Christian observer of the Northern
Ireland scene—if such is possible—it is clear that repentance
is a necessary response from all parties involved in the
conflict—British, Ulster Protestant and Irish Catholic.
Repentance needs to be both personal and communal.
Repentance at its simplest is saying, 'I am sorry, please
forgive me,' and, 'We are sorry, please forgive us.' It is one
of the hardest things for a human being to say—it seems
even harder for a community to enter into such repentance.
One of the most basic problems, assuming that we have
seen the need for repentance, is our tendency to feel that the
other person has transgressed more, and must therefore
repent first. When each party says that of the other there
can be no repentance, therefore no forgiveness, no reconciliation, no peace and no joy. That is the situation in
Northern Ireland.

It is essential that someone makes the first move because
resentment or an unforgiving spirit is one of the most
destructive forces in man. It feeds our own fear which grows

like a cancer, and also locks the other party in their resentments. Yet we hesitate to make the first move. 'It will put me in the wrong and him in the right.' 'It will make me seem weak.' When we take the step of repentance we discover exactly the opposite to be true. We see others released to appreciate us, to accept our present concern as genuine, and to love us.

Lord Hylton, an English Roman Catholic, spelt out the central importance of repentance for Northern Ireland in a speech in the House of Lords:

> I see repentance as a turning away from our unsatisfactory past and present in a deliberate attempt to create a better future. It involves not only the abandoning of entrenched positions, but willingness to compromise and, in addition, qualities of vision, of imagination and of necessarily risky creativity.... I hope we in Britain will recognize that our involvement with Ireland over the centuries has caused great injustices and major suffering. I trust that we shall renounce all attitudes of superiority. Some of these still exist, as witness the contemporary Irish jokes that portray Irish people as brainless peasants. We need to accept the Irish as fully human and as being every bit as civilized as ourselves.... I come now to the churches throughout Ireland. With the help of their colleagues in Britain I suggest that they have much to contribute to the whole area of repentance. They will come to see that their past behaviour has exacerbated economic, political and constitutional difficulties. I shall give only two instances: first, the rigid Roman Catholic attitudes over mixed marriages; and secondly, the politico-religious stance of the Orange order in Northern Ireland. Repentance for the church I believe, means the giving up of attitudes and behaviour which generate fear among other denominations.[1]

This call to repentance was the central note of an all Ireland rally held in Downpatrick in June 1981. About seven thousand Catholics and Protestants joined in prayers of repentance. It was a public acknowledgement of what is necessary at individual and community level all over the country.

Cecil Kerr spelt out the significance of such a public event:

This is not a triumphalist rally. We have come to cry out to God, 'Spare your people; have mercy on this land.' Judgement begins at the house of God. We have come to share in what has happened in our land. As Christians we want to confess the fears and suspicions which have led to bitterness or hatred; the long-standing prejudices which have led at times to violence and murder; the pride and self-righteousness that have kept us apart.

True repentance brings joy and release. God's peace is built on his righteousness and truth. Too many people in this land want peace so that they can go on sinning more comfortably.

The world has watched the agony of this land. We have become a byword to the nations. We are a stumbling block to many and we have dishonoured the name of Christ. We have too easily confessed faith in Christ with our lips when our hearts have been full of hate. God is exposing the hypocrisy of our nominal Christianity. He is calling us to a deep repentance.

Many are here who have been bereaved through violence. Many who have been deeply wounded by the hatred of others, have received from Christ a power to love and forgive. Some are here who were bitter and violent. Jesus Christ has changed our hearts. Those who were sworn enemies have embraced one another in the love of Christ. That's the miracle that God wants to repeat all over this land.

There is an urgency about the call to repentance in Northern Ireland, for it is here that the secure foundation for the future lies. Yet too many of us, for too long, have avoided this first step. We have been too adept at pointing out the faults of the other side, or, less blatantly, have thought only of the hurts that we have endured. There is very little in the teaching of Jesus that has more relevance to the Ulster problem than his teaching on the priority of repentance and reconciliation: 'If you are offering your gift at the altar, and there remember that your brother has something against you, leave your gift there before the altar and go; first be reconciled to your brother, and then come and offer your gift' (Mt 5:23–24).

When someone else has a grudge against me, like the Catholic Irish against the English, I must go and put it right—even if it causes some embarrassment. What will my friends say when I leave my gift at the altar and go off—will they not think I am taking things a little too seriously, making too much of a fuss? Will they not try and show me that it is not my problem if he feels sore at me? Will they not assure me that my going to him will only make him embarrassed, will make the whole situation worse? Will they not suggest to me that time is the greatest healer? Yes, many will say that, but they would all be wrong. The teaching of Jesus is that if my brother is upset or offended or resentful on account of me then his feelings are a priority. It suggests that we should first consider the need for the British to repent for what has been hurtful in their involvement in Ireland.

1. The British

We, the English, are the ones who should take the lead. I say this for several reasons. First, because I am English, and we should remove first the beam from our own eye; we should take the initiative in repentance. I cannot even begin to ask others to repent if I have not personally faced my own need to do so. Secondly, because history shows in the very broadest terms, 'We started it.' We should not haggle over details: we should accept our share and begin to bring release into the present situation by taking the first step. Thirdly, because it is easier for *us*. While it is true that we have lost many British soldiers in Ulster, we are far less caught up in the conflict than the Irish are—in fact we usually manage to live unaware of its existence for weeks on end.

The history itself, not to mention the TV documentaries about the Anglo-Irish question, makes plain the many causes for repentance. Soon after these TV documentaries were shown in 1980 a leading Christian minister from England who was speaking at an ecumenical renewal conference in Belfast confessed that, after watching them, it almost made him feel ashamed to be English. To repent of that past is the first step—and it is one that is demanded of the English. And this is not just a historical exercise to clear our 'national conscience'. The past is still having its effect in Ulster, and so our repentance of the past brings immediate release to the present. We repent of course, not only to release the injured party, but also because *we* are guilty and *we* need to be forgiven.

1981 was a grim year in Ulster. It was the year dominated by the hunger strike with its ten deaths. For everyone in Ulster it was a harrowing experience. For me, as an Englishman, it brought the whole issue of Northern Ireland into stark relief. On several occasions during the hunger strike I was over in England and the relative lack of concern at what was happening in Ulster at the time shocked me and made me deeply ashamed. The experience of these months impressed upon me the prime need for repentance on the part of us English. I can best convey the experience by quoting two things which I wrote at the time.

First, I wrote an article in the *Church of England Newspaper* in an attempt to convey the issues as they appeared from the perspective of an Englishman living in Northern Ireland. Bobby Sands had just died, many thousands had attended his funeral, and shops and businesses were closed as a mark of respect. (Many shopkeepers had been threatened and intimidated by the Provisionals to make sure they closed.)

The strong feelings of outrage and the anti-British outcry engendered around the world by the death of Bobby Sands were more significant than people in Britain realized.

At about that time I was in England and it was noticeable how little of that international feeling was reported in the British media.... I believe the duty of every Christian in the different camps is twofold—to seek a deep understanding of the other sides, and to ask first of one's own camp, 'How can *we* change in order to help the situation?'

My personal response as an Englishman must be to ask, 'Does my camp, the British, show understanding, are we open to change in our attitude at all?' At the moment I believe the answer is largely 'No.'

Increasingly I see emerging with the present government a specifically British view, detached and rather self-righteous, which suggests a lack of understanding both of the Unionist and Nationalist position here.

I see even less understanding of the Nationalist view—and here I'm in grave danger of being misunderstood! I deplore the murder of British soldiers and the police; I believe violence to be wrong as well as counter-productive; I believe that as long as Northern Ireland remains part of the United Kingdom any terrorist killing must be regarded as a criminal offence rather than an act of war, and therefore the government is right not to grant political status.

But, what is clear is that many now in the Maze prison would not be there were it not *for* the political situation. There are some who would be violent criminals even in a just society, but many more see themselves as fighting in the last round of the liberation battle against British occupation.

The British government must uphold the rule of law, but it must also show more understanding and flexibility and, I believe, be more anxious to receive any help from outside that is in a position to be more impartial.[2]

Living through the hunger strike forced me to see that it is not only past attitudes and actions of which we British need to repent but also similar thinking which still dominates present government attitudes. It is usually unpopular to challenge British anti-republican measures in Ulster—it is thought to be unpatriotic. But to be patriotic can sometimes be a very evil thing—if the government is wrong then to follow their lead, however patriotic, is to be duped by satanic deception. It is easy to acknowledge the many 'imperialist' mistakes of *former* British governments; it is the task of the confessing Christian church to recognize these mistaken attitudes when they appear in the *present*. I have no doubt that future historians will be pointing out what was unacceptable in the British government's attitude at the time of the Hunger Strike. Christians must have the moral courage to make such judgements at the time.

These thoughts were uppermost in my mind in May/June 1981. It was at that time that I felt it important to prepare the following statement for my fellow Christians in Northern Ireland—both Catholic and Protestant. With the advantage of hindsight I would still stand by what I said then.

As an Englishman, I have lived and worked for the past eighteen months in the Christian Renewal Centre at Rostrevor. I also have to ask myself about repentance. What do I and my people the English, need to repent of when we think of Ireland? I am aware that most of my fellow countrymen would say, 'Nothing!' At one time, I myself may have said something similar.

But there is much of which we as Englishmen need to repent, for the situation in Ireland is, to a large extent, due to the policies of British administrations through the centuries. But then, our history books which we have read in school for decades have not told us all the facts. They mentioned the potato famine in passing perhaps, but it was all very remote— there was no mention of the indifference of the British Government. Further back in the books, there was a lot about Oliver Cromwell, but they never said what happened at Drogheda.

There's plenty more, and we need to repent of those things in our past which have contributed to the distress of this land. There is no way in which I can represent anyone other than myself in this regard, but *I* want to say that I do have a deep sorrow in my heart over so much that has happened in the hundreds of years of English rule in Ireland.

But, I also realize that anything that happened in Ireland before 1969 is very little known in my home country. Consequently, it can seem a bit unreal to ask people to repent of things of which they are unaware—and if they knew of them would likely disapprove. What is far more real—and, I believe, far more urgent, is that we repent of our wrong attitudes *today*.

Just yesterday, God turned my thoughts to the parable of the Pharisee and the tax-collector. The Pharisee who, in his self-righteousness, stood and prayed thus with himself, 'God, I thank thee that I am not like other men.' I love my own people, but I have to say that if there is one sin which comes so easily to us, it is self-righteousness—a kind of national superiority has been bred over the years—a thousand years unconquered and many centuries as a world power have done a lot to promote a kind of smugness, the feeling that we know best. Perhaps it leads to the tendency to act without taking too much trouble to listen to what others think, or to understand how they feel.

I was in England for a few days recently—I was there when Bobby Sands died. Sadly, I noticed then this self-righteousness. It makes many try to forget the troubles in Northern Ireland, to pretend that it has nothing to do with them—and I see this both in Christians and non-Christians. It leads, in others, to a hardline approach; to be unyielding; to feel affronted and adopt positions of moral superiority; to show inflexibility and stand aloof, rather than realizing the responsibility we share for what is going on here. It is of this self-righteousness that I believe God is calling us as Englishmen to repent. I was heartened the other day to hear the Archbishop of Canterbury say in Dublin that he believed the British Government could find ways of acting more flexibly. I see that as a step in a godly direction.

I say all this, not because I don't love my own country, but because I do! I love Ireland also. But self-righteousness always keeps us from knowing God's blessing. It was so with the self-righteous Pharisee in the Temple—he went home far away from God. Whenever we say, 'I am in the right, it is the other person who must change, for there is nothing in me that is wrong,' then we distance ourselves from God. If you as an Irish Catholic, or an Irish Protestant say to the English, '*You* must change, not me,' that could breed a self-righteousness in you. We must stop telling each other to repent and repent ourselves. That's why I as an Englishman must first of all repent of the many wrong attitudes and actions of my people—and pray for a change of heart in ourselves, our government, and my fellow Christians over the water.

I am grateful to a Roman Catholic priest who pointed me to the very heart of repentance in Northern Ireland. 'All violence is wrong; it causes such tremendous destruction,' he said, 'but, could it be possible for you, as an Englishman who loves Jesus Christ, to say when a man from the IRA kills a British soldier, "Father forgive *me* for the hatred in the heart of that young man in the IRA which has so destroyed him that he went out and murdered another young man. Could you ever arrive at that kind of love that Jesus shows us? It is the kind of love that will save Ireland.'

Perhaps a good starting point is to remember St Patrick, the Patron Saint of Ireland, for he too was British. Fifteen hundred years ago he crossed the Irish Sea to bring Christ to Ireland—he loved the people of that land. It is only as we find that love in our hearts for the people of Ireland that we will take that step of repentance, the step that can bring release into the situation.

I remember vividly the release that came through one such act of repentance. I was leading an ecumenical service with repentance as its theme. A Roman Catholic priest had emphasized the bondage and oppression that his people felt because of the years of British rule. He said that repentance by the English could bring a much needed release to many Roman Catholic Christians in Ireland. After his talk it was important for me, as the English Chairman of the meeting, to make the right response. I had prepared nothing beforehand—it was one of those occasions when God speaks and puts you on the spot! I searched my own heart and felt that I had, on several occasions, made plain my own repentance and had confessed on my own part and on the part of my country's past and continuing injustices. I felt the freedom of forgiveness. Yet I was aware that of the several hundred Catholics there, many were locked in the oppressed feeling that 'the Brits' still held to the old desire to dominate, and were still unrepentant about the past. Consequently every present British action, however noble and disinterested, was tarred with past mistakes—because the power of the past had not been broken by repentance.

Though it was far from easy I stepped forward to the microphone and said that, as the first response, I would like to lead the few English people there (probably about a dozen) in an act of repentance on our behalf and in the name of all that has been, and is still, wrong in the English attitude. It was a very traumatic event and was not followed by immediate euphoria and rejoicing. I wondered, 'Have I confessed too much by going first? Have I made my own people seem blacker than they are?' Others who had made confession from their perspective were having similar feelings. 'Will the fact that I have confessed make the others presume on us?' The act of communal repentance is a very exposing event.

Over the next few days, however, the results began to show. One by one several Roman Catholics said to me what a great release they had felt when, for the first time, they had heard repentance on behalf of British rule down the centuries. I reflected that it had not made me feel any better. I had previously been released from my own sense of guilt. Confession is good for the soul but, as I learnt on this occasion, the 'good' done is sometimes not to the one who

repents but to those who are liberated on hearing that
confession.

2. The Ulster Protestant

In many ways the most fraught area in this call to repentance
can be seen in the position of the Ulster Protestants. Are they
the offending party or the injured party? The straightforward
case is that, ever since the Plantations of James I, the Protestants have built up a considerable record of unjust
domination: in the fifty years of Unionist ascendancy
following partition their record on Civil Rights was plainly
unjust. That is the simple way of looking at the facts. It is
the basic way; the honest way. The only response is for
Protestants to step out in the love of Christ and say, 'We're
sorry, please forgive us.'

There have been those who have done so. When the Civil
Rights campaign began in the late sixties, a number of
Protestant churchmen took a courageous lead by acknowledging the mistakes of their community throughout the
years of the Unionist Ascendancy. A leading Presbyterian
clergyman wrote to the newspaper in October 1968, 'We
cannot evade the truth that for years we have known of
various forms of social injustice and political discrimination
within our community and that we have found it mentally
more comfortable, politically more acceptable and socially
more convenient to acquiesce in these things.'[3] Sadly it was
a case of too little too late for the minority community. Had
the Unionists begun to repent of their disregard for injustice
before being forced into it by Catholic pressure (plus a
belated push from the Westminster Government) recent
history may well have been very different. Repentance, of
course, involves deeds to give force to the words—it would
have meant, much earlier, an end to gerrymandering, and
the establishing of equality of opportunity in housing and

jobs. In the event, both deeds and words came too late. But the force of history still demands this attitude of repentance from Ulster Protestants.

To the majority of Protestants, however, it does not seem as simple as that! Although words of repentance in 1968 were too little and too late for the minority community, they were clearly too much and too soon for a significant section within the Unionist camp who resisted any institutional repentance on behalf of the Unionist Ascendancy and its record over the previous fifty years. This Protestant un- willingness to repent, so reprehensible in 1968, has now spread to the majority of that community. It is difficult to judge it so harshly today.

Throughout the present troubles the Protestant com- munity have come to see themselves as an innocent group of people whose birthright is being snatched from them by brutal and subhuman terrorist atrocities. It would be hard to find words strong enough to express the injury and outrage that so many feel as a result of the IRA terrorist campaign of the seventies and eighties. 'How can we be expected to repent in the face of such brutality?' Thus, a community who base an understanding of their *rights* on a longer view of history see the question of who should repent first from a much shorter perspective. It is easy to challenge such a double-think on the grounds of logic and strict justice, but not so easy on the basis of the more emotional and immediate consideration of human sorrow and tragedy.

This aspect of repentance is charged with more emotion when we acknowledge the links between the Ulster Protes- tants and the British. Although the British, as we have already seen, have not shown clear evidence of repentance, there are those who have. Where it happens most is in the media—the television documentary providing the most obvious platform for such expression of British acknow- ledgement of past sins. It is part of our repentance for an imperial past which has been a feature of the liberal post-imperial age. We have seen so much of 'Empire' go in the last thirty years that we have become accustomed to acknowledging the 'more regrettable' parts of our imperialistic record.

To acknowledge, in this way, as most TV documentaries have done, the sins of Britain in Ireland usually involves confessing on their behalf the failure of the Ulster Protestant majority to govern their land on the basis of equal justice for all. The Protestant feels deserted and stabbed in the back by the British. The TV documentary may be right, but it is easy to repent of 'past-imperialism' when one sits securely in the freedom of an England who has left that past behind. But the Ulster Protestant is still living in the presence of past imperialist policies—a much less comfortable place to be. As Englishmen, we should be careful not to do other people's repenting for them, without acknowledging the far greater difficulty of their position.

But having said all this, Ulster Protestants have cause to repent. They are not confessing to the bombers in the IRA but to a community who have been unfairly treated down the centuries to such a degree that part of the result of that history has been a violent terrorist campaign by a small minority within their community. At the same time Protestants need to repent on behalf of those in their own community who have resorted to violence and killed many innocent Roman Catholics during the present conflict.

Again, such repentance must be more than words, it must issue in a stand against any activity within ones own community which perpetrates the old sectarianism. Consequently, when Paisley's Third Force was launched at the end of 1981, a clear challenge faced many Protestant clergy: would they publicly disassociate themselves from it? Paisley has an enormous following: it is often dynamite to criticize him publicly; there are many ministers who have lost dozens, even hundreds, to the Free Presbyterians for daring publicly to take a stand against 'Paisleyism'. But this is an essential part of repentance, and the emergence of the Third Force brought the issue to a head. Would ministers denounce all forms of violence—even that of the Third Force which was formed to defend the Protestant community more effectively than the security forces were doing? It was a particularly crucial time for the Presbyterian Church. Dr Grivan, the Moderator, gave a firm lead: 'Murder is murder, from whatever source it comes, and I would encourage our people not to be led by anyone along that road. It is a road which leads to hopelessness.' This was an unequivocal call not to join or support any of the vigilante groups of the Third Force.

The Belfast Telegraph realized the importance of Dr Grivan's stand. In an editorial, they welcomed this new departure.

> Not before time a Presbyterian leader is directly challenging Mr Paisley, and the implications of his policies. The battle is on, not only for the heart of Unionism, but also for the soul of Presbyterianism.... Dr Grivan's statement has given a clear lead, which other Protestant clergy can build upon.

A similar, and even more 'delicate' area is the importance of the Orange Order. Perhaps the action of Bishop Cuthbert Peacocke should be copied by many more clergy. On his enthronement as the Church of Ireland Bishop in Derry he resigned from the Orange Order, thus breaking his links with an organization that stands for Protestant Ascendancy. Not as many clergy are members of the order today as in previous decades but it is still widespread, and most, if not all, Protestant congregations in Ulster have some men who are members—in some cases nearly all the men in a congregation will be members. Gallagher and Worrall explain the problem about the continuing existence of the Orange Order:

> The Orange Order is an obstacle to peace in so far as it ensures that the majority of the majority, for which it speaks, maintain a rigid stance. It articulates their underlying fears in such a way as to suggest that there is only one way of guarding against dangers: obstinate resistance rather than mutual accommodation.[4]

It would be unfair to give the impression that all about the Order is wrong for it has many good points about it. It is officially against injustice to Roman Catholics and it provides many good and harmless opportunities for communal celebration. It is its indelible links with the notions of militant Protestant history and ascendancy over the Catholic community that make it a continual irritant to community reconciliation.

3. The Irish Catholic

It is a little short of presumptuous for an English Protestant to point out to an Irish Catholic his need of repentance. I only presume to do so because I believe that many of *us* (Protestant English) can be released into repentance for *our* sins by witnessing repentance within an Irish Roman Catholic. When he repents I see the love of Christ in him and that challenges me to consider whether that same divine love is at work in me. It is the Christian, be he Catholic or Protestant, who first accepts the call to repent that can be used of God to release others to enter similarly into repentance.

The Ulster Protestant is most helped to repent if Catholics acknowledge and repent of the evil and violence perpetrated in their name by members of republican paramilitary groups. Again, deeds should follow words and this must mean that no Catholic who thus repents should withhold information that will lead to the apprehension of anyone who commits terrorist offences. The same, of course, is true for Protestants in relation to 'their' paramilitaries. There is no denying the cost involved in doing this.

Father Jim Burke, an Irish American Catholic Priest, in a talk on repentance at the Christian Renewal Centre spoke of the Catholic Church's 'imperial' attitudes towards other denominations.

> There is a tremendous repentance needed by us Catholics. We have such an enormous feeling of superiority within us with regard to our Church. It means that many of us won't listen to a Protestant minister. We always see him as inferior to a priest. When we can't receive such a brother and listen to him as a messenger from God then we have become like the Pharisees in Jesus' day. We must say, 'Lord I'm sorry for looking down on others. I'm sorry for thinking I have all the truth.' What is the truth, anyway? The truth is a person—Jesus Christ. Have you got all of Jesus? When you ask me, 'Do we have all the truth, Father?' my answer is one word—NO!

My own response to these words, when I first heard them, was one of tremendous release. I had several times experienced the pain of rejection by Roman Catholics whom I had got to know as brothers and sisters in Christ. There have been times when some have made it plain that if the crunch comes a Protestant minister is always inferior to a Catholic priest whatever the relative quality of their life and ministry might be. I, as a Protestant, was blessed by a Catholic's repentance of his Church's 'superiority complex'.

All of us have much to gain by taking risks in repentance. So many log-jammed situations are freed; so many past wounds are healed; so many new relationships are formed and mistrust is banished 'at a stroke'. There can be few things the devil likes less than when God's people take repentance seriously!

9. A Question of Identity

At the heart of the Irish problem lies the question of identity. 'How do I see myself?' 'How do I describe myself?'

The British are confused about this Irish question of identity, because it is a different one from our own. For centuries a person's individual identity within England has been based on class distinctions. In these more secular times professing Christians have become much more aware of their identity as God's people in an ungodly society. Even more recently, identity has been defined by some on the basis of the colour of a person's skin.

These three are not fundamental to the Irish awareness of identity. In Ireland, and particularly in Ulster, there are two basic questions. Which religion are you? What nationality are you?

Are you Prod or Taig?

That is the colloquial way of enquiring about a person's religion—Protestant or Catholic? Even more cryptically—'which foot?' This comes from the distant agricultural past of Ireland. The English settlers used spades with a shoulder to the right and thus dug with their right foot; the native Irish, on the other hand, used spades with a shoulder on the left hand side.

In Northern Ireland, however it is asked, this question is of fundamental importance. For many people, it is the first thing they want to know on meeting someone new. It will often define whether or not they are likely to trust one another. This denominational background is usually far more significant than an individual's personality.

There is a popular joke told in Belfast which highlights the importance of this issue. An incomer is being questioned by some locals. 'Are you a Catholic or a Protestant?' they ask. 'Neither,' comes the reply, 'I am a Jew.' 'Well,' they insist, 'are you a Catholic Jew or a Protestant Jew?' Everyone has to be one or the other. Whether or not an individual attends church makes very little difference. The issue centres on the religious tradition into which one was born.

When I first moved to live in Northern Ireland this was one of the most difficult 'lessons' I had to learn. Whether I was a Protestant or Catholic seemed more important than whether or not I was a Christian. The secondary identity has assumed precedence over the fundamental identity.

Are you British or Irish?

The Ulster Protestant has no doubt about his religious identity. He is Protestant and is proud of it. He is sure he is right and he will go to all lengths to defend it. There is a determined certainty about his Protestant identity. But there, often, the certainty ends and the basic insecurity begins. The Northern Ireland Protestant has fundamental doubts about his nationality.

This first occurred to me when I was spending an evening at the home of some Christian friends in Belfast. They are Christians whom I admire for the way they have responded to the move of God's Spirit in Ireland. Although they both come from very staunch East Belfast Protestant stock we have on many occasions shared fellowship together with

Roman Catholics in evangelistic and renewal meetings. They have left far behind the old sectarian attitudes that prescribe how God should work.

In the course of our conversation I referred to Adrian and Janice as 'Irish'. They quickly put me right. They had never considered themselves Irish—nor, to their knowledge, did any of their Protestant friends. 'Then what are you?' I asked. 'We are British,' they affirmed, 'but, of course, when we're over the water we want to emphasize our difference from the English and so we say that we're from Northern Ireland.'

This basic confusion of identity affects the majority of Ulster Protestants. An Englishman can say, 'First I am English, then I am British.' The Scot will say, 'First, and most important of all, I am a Scot; secondly I am British.' The Welsh say something similar. Catholics in Ireland, North and South, proudly affirm, 'We're Irish.' Many Protestants in Northern Ireland say, 'I'm British'—and that is a very unsatisfactory basis for a national identity.

John Dunlop, a Presbyterian minister expresses well this basic problem of his own people.

> If any single concept could describe the corporate consciousness of Protestants in Northern Ireland it remains that of a community under siege. We have always been an insecure people. Threatened by the Catholic Irish, we have retreated within the physical, mental, emotional, cultural and religious borders of the North. We are dominated by what we are not. We are not Catholic and not Irish. We say we are British but that is only partly true and is in reality only a way of defending ourselves against the threat of being swallowed up by Catholic Ireland.... A people who define themselves in terms of what they are not, are not a free people. A church which is obsessed by what it is not has not entered into the freedom offered in Christ.[1]

It is not possible to 'share power' or be reconciled with Roman Catholics on such an insecure foundation. It means there is the ever-present fear of a Catholic takeover. The greatest need for the Ulster Protestant is to discover a positive sense of identity which will enable him to leave behind his defensive past. There are two ways in which this can be achieved—one in terms of a new national identity, the other in terms of a deep awareness of our identity as children of God.

There is an emerging sense of 'Ulster-identity'. It is probably being forced on people by the growing feeling that they can no longer rely on any long term commitment from the British Government. This at any rate was the conclusion of the St Patrick's Day reflections of leading Ulster journalist, Alf McCreary.

> I am constantly amazed by the number of Unionists who talk disparagingly in private about 'the Brits'. There is a growing Northern Irish identity which only the blind refuse to see. It is not a tangible political identity in the form of a significant move towards Ulster's independence. But it is a stirring beneath the surface, a grudging realization that neither London nor Dublin really understands the North and that the Ulsterman ultimately can be his own best friend, or as has happened, his own worst enemy.[2]

Although this has not yet meant a significant number wanting independence, this trend, if it develops, will most likely lead to some kind of independence for Northern Ireland. Or rather, some form of interdependence within a wider, British, Irish or European context.

But such thoughts are mere speculations about a far off political solution. In the meantime the resolution of this question of identity does not have to sit back and wait for that indefinite future. It is the work of the Holy Spirit to give us such a deep awareness of our identity as children of God, that confusion about our secondary identity becomes insignificant by comparison.

According to St Paul our basic freedom lies in our awareness that we are God's children, heirs together with Christ. There is no greater dignity, nor more secure position than that. No worldly wealth can buy such security, and no human family has such a status. There is no more fundamental understanding of nationality than one's awareness of being part of God's own people. It is the work of God's Spirit within us that brings such security. It is God's Spirit that enables us to cry, 'Abba! Father!' (cf. 1 Pet 2:9–10; Rom 8:14–17).

This is why Adrian and Janice are secure enough to share openly in fellowship with Roman Catholic Christians. The inbred uncertainty about their Irishness or their Britishness does not affect them fundamentally because, through the work of God's Spirit, they are secure in their identity as God's children. It is this security that lies at the heart of all true reconciliation.

We must resist all attempts to define us in other ways. We must not allow secondary identities to govern our relationship with others. In Ireland I relate to a fellow Roman Catholic Christian on the basis of our common sonship and not on the basis of my Protestantism or his Catholicism. In England I relate to a West Indian Christian on the basis of our being heirs together with Christ which has nothing at all to do with the colour of our skins. This is the only secure foundation for reconciliation within the body of Christ.

During the period of the hunger strike in 1981, this truth was impressed upon me very forcefully. Because I was living in an area which is 90% republican most of the Christians I knew in the locality were Roman Catholics. I had come to love them and greatly value their fellowship but while the hunger strike was going on in the Maze prison, I began to notice difficulties intruding into my relationships with one or two Catholic Christian friends. I was confused by this, and so were they, as I later discovered.

I was aware that many republicans were inevitably finding it more difficult to relate to an Englishman during this period. I noticed that people serving me in a shop would not speak to me on discovering I was English. I understood this and realized it was an inevitable part of the heightened 'anti-Brit' feeling that was caused by the H-block situation. I believed that it was an intensity of feeling that would die down when the hunger strike ended and I, like other Englishmen in Northern Ireland, would have to wait for that change to happen, and pray that it would happen soon.

All that I understood and accepted. What I could neither understand nor accept was the growing coolness in relationship between myself and a few Roman Catholic Christians with whom previously I had shared close fellowship. I 'knew' that I felt no different towards them, and I could not imagine why they should be changing in their attitude towards me. After a few weeks of 'being sent to Coventry', I began to respond in the same way!

It was a thoroughly disorientating experience. I found it affected deeply my own relationship with God: prayer became extremely difficult. We could not understand why things were as they were and we seemed at first powerless and then, later, unwilling, to do anything about it.

With the advantage of hindsight it seems amazing that we were so dull and slow to understand. What had happened was that we were still trying to relate to each other as Christians but we were failing because a subtle difference had entered into that relationship. They were relating to me as a *British* Christian and I was relating to them as *Irish Republican* Christians. There was a confusion about our identity. We had allowed secondary identities to intrude and we had lost the freedom of our unity in Christ because we had, temporarily, lost the basis on which it is founded. That freedom returned when we realized what had happened; when we saw that we had fallen prey to one of the most insidious of demonic stratagems—we had begun to relate on the basis of secondary identities.

A song I have often sung in gatherings of Catholic and Protestant Christians in Ireland expresses this fundamental truth which we need constantly to affirm—and equally ensure that it, and it alone remains the basis of our understanding of ourselves and of our fellow Christians.

> We are heirs of the Father
>   We are joint heirs with the Son
> We are children of the Kingdom
>   We are family, we are one![3]

One day, there will be a political solution that will help to solve the secondary problem of national identity. Meanwhile, we must pray that there will be such a mighty outpouring of the Spirit of God that many thousands will discover an unchallengeable security in their primary, fundamental identity as children of God. On this basis Ulster Protestant, Irish Catholic and British Christian can relate without fear as members of one family, as children of the one Father, 'from whom every family in heaven and on earth is named' (Eph 3:15).

Notes

Chapter 1

1. Fianna Fail and Fine Gael are the two major parties in the parliament of the Irish Republic, The Dail (pronounced 'Doyle').

Chapter 2

1. Robert Kee, *Ireland: A History,* London 1980, p. 248.
2. Antonia Fraser, *King James I.*
3. Robert Kee, op. cit., p. 42.
4. *Ireland: Land of Troubles,* London 1979, p. 195.
5. Edmund Spenser, *A View of the State of Ireland in 1596.*

Chapter 3

1. John Dunlop, 'Pastoral Dimensions in the Northern Ireland Conflict', *The Furrow,* January 1982.
2. Mary Grant, *Journey Into Hope,* Belfast 1980, p. 33.

Chapter 4

1. Quoted by Ron Wilson, *A Flower Grows in Ireland,* David C. Cook Publishing Co., Illinois 1974, p. xii.
2. Ian Willis, *Church of England Newspaper,* November 20th 1981.
3. Ron Wilson, op. cit., pp. 131-32.

4. 'Ireland's Divided Disciples', *The Furrow*, January 1982, p. 23.

5. I am aware that the use of the word 'fundamentalist' can be misleading. I use it because it is the one most often used by others in Northern Ireland to describe the section of the community with which I am dealing here. It is not, of course, used simply to describe those who, as conservative Evangelicals, believe in the supreme authority of Scripture and are committed to evangelism. It is used to describe those who hold to the interpretation of Christianity as evidenced within the Free Presbyterian Church—but many who hold such views are still members of other denominations. The word 'Paisleyites' is used by many but this tends to describe the more exclusively political aspects of their position and not necessarily the 'spiritual heart'. There are many, of course, who are politically Paisleyite but who do not subscribe to all the spiritual foundations of the movement.

6. Eric Gallagher and Stanley Worrall, *Christians in Ulster 1968-1980*, Oxford 1982, p. 24.

7. Ron Wilson, op. cit., pp. 27-28.

8. *The Revivalist*, April 1966.

9. 'H-Block and Its Background', *Doctrine and Life*, November 1980.

10. *The Coming Revolution*, 1913. For these references to Padraig Pearse's writings I am indebted to Professor Lyons' book, *Ireland Since the Famine*.

11. 'Ghosts', written in 1915 and published in *Political Writings and Speeches*, Dublin 1922, p. 226.

12. *Political Writings and Speeches*, Dublin 1922, pp. 215-18.

Chapter 5

1. Jim Wallis, *A Call to Conversion*, Lion Publishing 1981, p. 6.

2. Ron Wilson, op. cit., p. 131.

Chapter 6

1. Cecil Kerr, *Power to Love*, Belfast 1976, p. 111.
2. Graham Kendrick, *Jesus Stand Among Us*, Copyright ©
1977 Thankyou Music, P.O. Box 75, Eastbourne BN23 6NW.
Used by permission.

Chapter 7

1. Ibid, pp. 97-99.
2. Ibid, p. 121.

Chapter 8

1. Lord Raymond Hylton, House of Lords Debate,
November 5th 1981.
2. *Church of England Newspaper*, June 12th 1981.
3. The Rev. Carlisle Patterson in the *Newsletter*, October
15th 1968.
4. Eric Gallagher and Stanley Worrall, *Christians in Ulster
1968-1980*, Oxford 1982, pp. 197-98.

Chapter 9

1. John Dunlop, 'Pastoral Dimensions in the Northern
Ireland Conflict', *The Furrow*, January 1981, pp. 39-40.
2. Belfast Telegraph, St Patrick's Day, March 17th 1982.
3. Jimmy and Carol Owens, *We Are Heirs of the Father*,
Lexicon Music, Box 296, Woodland Hills, CA. 91365, USA.
Used by permission.

The Spirit of Renewal

by Edward England

What has the charismatic movement done for the church?

This is a unique survey of the events and controversies surrounding this exciting move of God's Spirit from the early sixties through to the eighties. Here are the stories of renewed Christians and renewed churches.

Based on the first 100 issues of *Renewal* magazine this is a vivid portrayal of the blessings and the tensions—dealing with such vital issues as prophecy, praise, tongues, evangelism, social action, Christian unity, and conflict with the 'establishment'.

Edward England, formerly Religious Publishing Director of Hodder and Stoughton, is now the publisher of *Renewal*. The editor is Michael Harper.

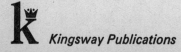

Kingsway Publications